▶ FOCUS ON ◀

Advanced
English

C.A.E. PRACTICE TESTS
WITH GUIDANCE

REVISED EDITION

LONGMAN

SUE O'CONNELL

Pearson Education Limited
Edinburgh Gate
Harlow
Essex CM20 2JE
England

ISBN 0 582 38258 0

Set in Minion
Printed in Spain by Graficas Estella

Author's Acknowledgements
Special thanks go to my friend Sue Scott of Brunel College, Bristol for her invaluable comments and suggestions. Thanks are also due to those who helped with the recordings: Bob Mills, Mary Dallas, Chris Dibden, Brian Janes, Clare McDowell, Brent Merrylees, Peter and Linda Newberry, Sue Scott, Julia Simnet.

We are grateful to the following for permission to reproduce copyright material:

the author, Jane Bidder for an extract from her article 'How to win Prizes for Keeping Quiet' in *THE TIMES*; the author, Michael Booth for an adapted extract from his article 'The quiet crusaders' in *THE SUNDAY TELEGRAPH* 31.5.98; Bristol City Council/ Bristol Tourism and Conference Bureau for extracts from 'Bristol Harbour' and 'Back-chat' by Karen Jamieson in *BRISTOL OFFICIAL VISITORS GUIDE*; *CARA* the inflight magazine of *AER LINGUS* for an extract from the article 'Oscar's Winning Performance' by Lorna Siggins in *CARA* November/December 1992; Ewan MacNaughton Associates for an extract from 'The squeaky clean chemist' by Anthony Daniels in *THE SUNDAY TELEGRAPH* 18.10.98 © Telegraph Group Ltd. London 1998; Express Newspapers for an adapted extract from '...Or having a ball?' and 'The real thing' from "The Health Promotion Feature" in *THE SUNDAY EXPRESS MAGAZINE* 5.4.92; the author, Mike Gerrard for his article 'Get that smell down on paper' in *THE SUNDAY TELEGRAPH*, Review 4.10.98; the author, Liz Gill for an extract from her article 'Curing the ill-mannered' in *THE TIMES* 4.5.89; Gruner & Jahr Ltd for extracts from 'Skiing at the limits' by Paula Reed and 'Adapting to the climate – cold comforts and hot sweats' in *FOCUS MAGAZINE* no 2, January 1993; Guardian News Services Ltd for an extracts from 'Car Chaos' by Mike Hamer in *THE NEW INTERNATIONALIST* May 1989 and 'Flying pigeons forever' in *THE NEW INTERNATIONALIST* January, 1993; the author, Nick Hanna for an extract from his article 'In search of the fish with the longest name' in *THE SUNDAY TIMES* 16.7.89; the author, Susan Hill for an extract from her article 'How to find out about dinosaurs' in *THE SUNDAY TIMES*, 6.10.91 © Susan Hill 1991; Home Office for an adapted extract reprinted and recorded from a leaflet on 'Practical Ways to Crack Crime'; Independent Newspapers Ltd for extracts from 'High-tech practice as the tutor preaches' by Karen Gold in *THE INDEPENDENT ON SUNDAY* 25.6.91 and 'Intruder that's a cause of alarm' by Helen Fielding in *THE INDEPENDENT ON SUNDAY* 8.5.92; the author, Christopher Matthew for an extract from his article 'Olympic Gold' in *HIGH LIFE MAGAZINE* July 1982; National Magazine Co Ltd for recipe for Tomato & Artichoke salad with basil' from *GOOD HOUSEKEEPING* May 1991. recording and tapescript. © Good Housekeeping Magazine; Oxford University Press for an extract from the 'Preface' in *TRAVELLERS' HEALTH* by Richard Dawood (1986); Reader's Digest Association for an extract from 'Feel Better Naturally' by Anita Bartholomew in *READER'S DIGEST* August 1998; Solo Syndication for an adapted extract from 'Careful, that mood may be catching' by Geraldine Bell in *THE EVENING STANDARD* 2.7.92 and an extract from 'How to have a baby and save your career' by Flora Hunter in *THE EVENING STANDARD* 4.9.91; Ewan MacNaughton Associates for an extract from 'The squeaky clean chemist' by Anthony Daniels in *THE SUNDAY TELEGRAPH* 18.10.98 © Telegraph Group Ltd. London 1998; the author, David Thomas for an extract from his article 'Look Daddy, I can fly' in *THE TIMES SATURDAY REVIEW* 6.6.92; Times Newspapers Ltd for extracts from the articles 'Service without a smile' by Tim Rayment & Philip Beresford in *THE TIMES* 8.10.89. 'Another cliff hanger' by Marcel Berlins in *THE TIMES*, 'Metro' supplement 30.10.89. 'Book reading a lost art at Harvard' by Charles Bremmer in *THE TIMES* 3.11.89. all © Times Newspapers Limited, 1989. 'Hotels pick up bills for five-star thieves' by Robin Young in *THE TIMES* 25.11.92. © Times Newspapers Limited, London 1992. 'There's plenty of room on planet Earth' by Nigel Hawkes in *THE TIMES* Supplement 28.4.98. 'The cost of getting lost' by Joe Warwick in *THE TIMES* 20.6.98. 'Guru to New York's pampered pooches' by Andrew Morgan in *THE TIMES* 4.7.98. 'How to help parents cope with homework' by John O'Leary in *THE TIMES* September 1998. 'Homework' in *THE TIMES* 1998, 'The direct approach' by Guy Walters in *THE TIMES*, October 1998. 'The ideal home that collapsed in minutes' by 'A correspondent' in *THE TIMES* 14.10.98. 'TV on-off switch may help to save planet' by Nick Nuttall and Roland Watson in *THE TIMES* 26.10.98. all © Times Newspapers Limited, 1998. 'Software Review' by James Cahill in *THE TIMES*, Interface Supplement 14.10.98. © James Cahill/Times Newspapers Limited, 1998. 'Send in the Clowns' by John Naish in *THE TIMES* "This Life" supplement 24.10.98. © John Naish/Times Newspapers Limited, 1998; the author, Edward Walsh for an extract from his article 'Looking for special agents' by Edward Walsh in *THE SUNDAY TIMES* 26.2.89.

We have been unable to trace the copyright holders of 'Last flip of the brochure' by Tom Chesshyre and SECRETS OF TALKING YOUR WAY TO THE TOP by Philippa Davies and would appreciate any information which would enable us to do so.

Sample OMR answer sheets are reproduced by permission of *the University of Cambridge Local Examination Syndicate.*

We are grateful to the following for permission to reproduce photographs and other copyright material:

Aerofilms & Colour Library for 148 top and centre, 149 top and centre; Chatto & Windus for 152; from: Martin Parr, The Cost of Living, Cornerhouse Publications for 151; Dominic Photography for 121 bottom right; Greg Evans International for 121 top right, bottom left and bottom centre, 147 top centre and centre left; Robert Harding Picture Library for 14 centre; Innovations for 56, 147 bottom; News of the World Magazine, 21.2.1993 for 145 top; Pictor International for 121 top left and top centre, 147 top left and top right; Reed Consumer Books for 153, 154; Tony Stone Images for 29, 97(a),(b) and (c), 148 bottom; Sunday Express Magazine/Ian Dicks for 40; Telegraph Colour Library for 97(d), (e) and (f), 146 bottom; Thames & Hudson for 145 bottom, 146 top; Times Newspapers for 23(Joe), 77 (Barry Greenwood); Topham Picturepoint for 124; Don Wright Inc. for 46.

Illustrations by David Cook, Nick Hardcastle, Robert Kettel, Robert Goldsmith, Kim Lane, Trevor Ridley, Angela Wood

Project Managed by Helena Gomm

Contents

▶ Introduction

About this book

The aim of this book is to help you prepare as effectively as possible for the **Cambridge Certificate in Advanced English (CAE)**, and it is designed to be useful whether you are studying alone or attending a class. It includes five complete practice tests, modelled on the most recent CAE exams, and also provides an introduction to the exam and helpful advice on tackling each paper.

Test 1 is a guided test. This means that each of the five papers is introduced and explained, section by section, before you attempt it yourself. You are given examples of the main question types that you can expect to meet together with guidance on answering them. To help you further, there is an Answer Key to Test 1 on page 47.

Tests 2 and **3** have notes in the page margins to remind you of important points. These will help you to answer the questions and encourage you to approach the exam in the right way.

Tests 4 and **5** are exactly like real examination papers, with no guidance or reminders.

The material in this book has been chosen to represent the widest possible range of topics and styles and also to reflect the emphasis on authenticity in the CAE exam. Reading texts are mostly reproduced in their original format and, in keeping with Cambridge policy, the listening texts include a proportion of authentic recordings and a variety of accents.

Important: To get the most benefit from this book, work carefully through Test 1 to begin with, making sure you are familiar with the requirements of each paper. Only then should you go on to the other tests.

About the CAE exam

If you really want to pass an exam, it's important to know as much about the exam as possible. In this way you find out what to expect from the exam and, more importantly, what the examiners expect from you! This section will help you to increase your knowledge of the CAE exam and will answer many of the questions which students often want to ask when approaching the exam for the first time.

To see how well-informed you are about the CAE exam, try answering the short quiz below. You will find the answers when you read the information which follows.

How much do you know about CAE?		
1 The level of the exam is half way between First Certificate and Proficiency.	True ☐	False ☐
2 Each paper is worth 20% of the total marks.	True ☐	False ☐
3 You have to write your answers on a special answer sheet for		
Paper 1 Reading ☐ Paper 2 Writing ☐ Paper 3 English in Use ☐	Paper 4 Listening ☐	
4 You can take CAE in more than 60 countries.	True ☐	False ☐
5 Paper 1 (Reading) includes multiple choice vocabulary questions.	True ☐	False ☐
6 There are two tasks in Paper 2 (Writing).	True ☐	False ☐
7 You can choose to answer questions on set books in Paper 2.	True ☐	False ☐
8 Paper 3 (English in Use) includes a question where you have to correct grammar mistakes.	True ☐	False ☐
9 In Paper 4 (Listening), all the recordings are played twice.	True ☐	False ☐
10 For Paper 5 (Speaking), you may be examined individually or with another candidate.	True ☐	False ☐

Let's look at some of the typical questions which candidates ask about the CAE examination.

What level of English do I need for CAE?

The CAE is an **advanced level** exam and it is described by Cambridge as being two thirds of the way between First Certificate and Proficiency. Someone taking CAE therefore needs a good level of ability in the four language skills, listening, speaking, reading and writing and a good grasp of the main areas of grammar. But it is a practical rather than an academic exam and you will not need to deal with literary texts or understand very advanced or specialised vocabulary.

It's worth noting that there is a lot of reading to do in CAE (the texts in the Reading paper amount to approximately 3,000 words) so you will need to be a confident and efficient reader.

Who is it suitable for?

The CAE exam is designed as a high-level final qualification with an emphasis on real world, practical tasks. It is therefore suitable for people who want to use English for professional or study purposes, and it can also serve as a 'stepping-stone' for people who want to develop the language skills necessary for the Proficiency exam.

CAE is recognised by the majority of British universities for English language entrance requirements, and these are listed in the leaflet 'Recognition in Britain', which is available from UCLES, 1 Hills Road, Cambridge CB1 2EU.

What does CAE consist of?

These are the details of the five papers:

Paper 1 Reading 1 hour 15 minutes	There are four parts and approximately 45 questions which test different reading skills. Questions include various kinds of matching, gap-filling and multiple choice items. There are no multiple choice vocabulary questions.
Paper 2 Writing 2 hours	Two tasks of approximately 250 words each are set. The first is compulsory, the second is selected from a choice of four topics.
Paper 3 English in Use 1 hour 30 minutes	There are six parts and approximately 80 questions. These test the correct choice of grammar and vocabulary, the ability to identify and correct mistakes, word formation, the ability to adapt a text in a particular style, and also the ability to understand text structure.
Paper 4 Listening approx. 45 minutes	There are four parts and 30–40 questions which test a range of listening skills. One of the recordings is heard only once. Questions include various kinds of matching, completion and multiple choice items.
Paper 5 Speaking approx. 15 minutes	Candidates are examined in pairs by two examiners and there are four parts designed to test a wide range of speaking skills.

Notes: 1 For Papers 1, 3 and 4, the answers must be written on special answer sheets.
2 There are no set books or optional papers.

How many people take CAE every year? And how many of them pass?

The CAE examination was introduced in 1991 and it is now taken in about 1,000 examination centres throughout the world. In 1997, there were over 48,000 candidates for the CAE exam in about 67 countries.

The percentage of those who pass will vary each year, of course, but on average around 65–70% of those who take the exam can expect to pass it.

How many marks do I need to pass CAE?
There is no set pass mark but you would normally be expected to get about 60% in order to pass at Grade C. To allow for slight differences in the difficulty of the exam, the exact level needed for a Pass is only set after the papers have been taken.

Are all the papers equally important?
Yes. Each paper carries 20% of the marks. So, even though the Listening and Speaking papers are much shorter than the written papers, they are worth the same number of marks.

Is it necessary to pass every paper?
No. There are five papers and what counts is your overall score. So it's possible to fail a paper but still pass the exam as a whole if you do exceptionally well on the other papers. But you must sit all of the papers – being absent from any of the papers will automatically mean that you have to take the whole exam again at a future date.

How is the exam graded?
There are three Pass grades – A, B and C, and two Fail grades – D and E. Any result which is lower than grade E is unclassified. Certificates are issued to successful candidates and these show the overall grade. In addition, candidates receive results slips with an exam profile showing more details about their performance in individual papers.

Finally, let's look at the language used in CAE exam papers. Like most exams, CAE sometimes uses formal or specialised words in the instructions for questions. Look, for example, at the following instructions from a question in Paper 4:

*Choose the **correct option** from A, B, C or D.*

This could be 'translated' more simply as 'Choose the best answer'.

Here are some more examples from CAE papers. See if you can match the part in italics with one of the words or phrases below.

Do You Speak CAE?		
Paper 1	1	Answer the questions by ***referring to*** the newspaper article.
	2	***Indicate*** the letter A, B, C or D ***against*** the number of each question.
Paper 2	3	All tasks in this section ***carry*** equal marks.
	4	Write to your friend ***referring to*** the points in the letter.
	5	You should ***indicate*** which of the advertisements you feel to be most successful and why.
Paper 3	6	You must ***transfer*** your answers to the separate answer sheet.
	7	Complete the following ***extract*** from a letter of complaint ...
	8	The words you need do not ***occur*** in the formal letter.
Paper 4	9	You will hear five short ***extracts*** in which various people are talking ...
	10	Decide which one on the list each speaker is ***referring to***.

reading	next to	short section	talking about	copy
appear	say	recordings	are worth	write	mentioning

▶ Guidance
Practice Test 1
PAPER 1 READING

In this paper there are four parts and you will have four texts to read and about 45 questions to answer. The time allowed is 1 hour 15 minutes, and during that time you also have to transfer your answers on to a special answer sheet.

The paper contains three different kinds of question and these are described below. The important thing to remember is that you will need to approach each kind of question in a different way, using different reading skills. For some questions, you need to read the whole text very carefully, for example. For others, you only need to find the key information as quickly as possible. If you don't approach the questions in the right way, you won't finish the paper in the time allowed.

> **Tip**
> ▋ In the exam, it's best to transfer your answers to the answer sheet after you finish each part, rather than waiting till the end of the exam. Otherwise you may run out of time at the end.

Multiple Matching Questions (Parts 1 and 4)

In this task you are given a list of questions (**1, 2, 3**) and a list of possible answers (**A, B, C**) to choose from. If you look at the examples on pages 22 and 28 you will see that you have to use some answers more than once, and you may have to give more than one answer to a question.

There are multiple matching questions in both **Parts 1** and **4** but the text for **Part 4** is longer (up to 1,200 words) and there are usually more questions (up to 22), which you should remember when planning your exam strategy. Although the texts for these two parts can sometimes appear a bit long and complicated, you don't need to read the whole text in great detail and the questions are usually very straightforward.

> **Multiple Matching Questions: General Advice**
> 1 **Read the instructions very carefully** so you know exactly what you have to do.
> 2 **Glance at the text** – just to see what it's about and how it's organised.
> 3 **Look through the questions.** These will tell you what information to look for.
> 4 **Scan the text for the information you need** – it may be in the same words as the question but

more often it is expressed slightly differently, so you need to be on the look-out for this. Don't waste time on other parts of the text.

Gapped Text (Part 2)

In this task, which focuses on **text structure**, you are given a text with gaps in it and you have to choose from a list of possible paragraphs to fill each gap. There is an example on page 24.

To complete the task successfully, you need to understand the development of ideas, opinions or events. It is often considered one of the hardest questions in Paper 1 but, like any other question, you can make life easier if you approach it in the right way.

> **Gapped Text: General Advice**
> 1 **Read through the incomplete text first** so that you understand what the general meaning and structure is.
> 2 **Read the text more carefully.** Study the information before and after each gap and look for grammatical or logical clues which can help you find the missing pieces of the jigsaw.
> 3 **Cross off each paragraph you choose,** so that the choice becomes easier.
> 4 When you've finished, **check that the completed text makes good sense.**

Multiple Choice Questions (Part 3)

This is a very common kind of exam question where you are given a question or an unfinished statement and you have to select the best answer from four choices. There is an example on page 26.

> **Multiple Choice Questions: General Advice**
> 1 **Read the text quickly for general meaning** before you look at the questions. This will give you a general idea of the topic, the writer's point of view and how the text is organised.
> 2 **Don't worry about difficult vocabulary at this stage.** You might not need to understand it in order to answer the questions.
> 3 **Look through the questions** to see which parts of the text you need to read again more carefully. Try to **guess** what the right answer is at this stage – even if it's a wild guess, this will help you read more effectively later.
> 4 **Find those parts of the text** and then read them slowly and carefully.
> 5 Try to **work out the meaning of any words you don't know** by looking at the context.

Paper 1, Part 1

▶ Turn to **Part 1** on pages 22–23 and follow steps 1–3 of the General Advice to answer the questions below. Then follow step 4 to answer **questions 1–4** of the task before turning back to this page.

- What's the text about? What is the writer's purpose in writing it? to describe a journey? to entertain? to offer advice? to advertise a service?
- What do the instructions ask you to do?
- Can you remember any of the headings?

Remember that to answer this question effectively (and leave yourself enough time for the rest of the paper) you need to **scan** the text rather than read each section in great detail. The section headings may give you a clue about where to look first for some of the questions. For example, *other passengers* in questions 6 and 7 might lead you to section D *Make friends*, while *business class* in question 11 might lead you to section B *Fly economy class*.

For most of the questions in this task you need to look for words or phrases in the text which are another way of expressing the same information as in the question.

It's a good idea to think about any alternative expressions you know before you turn to the text.

Question 1: The word *clothes* is not used in the text, so you should look for any alternative word or example.
Question 2: Again, you won't find the general word *accident* and you need to find a specific example mentioned.
Question 3: What are the different parts of an airline seat, e.g. the back, the seat, the headrest ...?
Question 4: In this case, you will find the word *food* mentioned. What alternative expression is also used?

Answers:
1 E (*Batman costume*)
2 H (*the driver ran over a cow*)
3 B (*fixed armrests*)
4 A (*special meals/basic food*)

▶ Now complete the questions for **Part 1**. When you've finished, you can check your answers on page 47.

Paper 1, Part 2

▶ Turn to **Part 2** on page 24 and follow steps 1–3 of the General Advice to answer **questions 15** and **16**.

Once you've read through the incomplete text, look carefully at each gap, considering the information which comes both before and after, and looking for any logical or grammatical clues.

Question 15: There are links with the paragraph before as well as the one after. The first paragraph mentions a report on the subject of map-reading. The following paragraph refers to *the apparent male superiority in navigating*, which must refer to the same report (*navigating* = finding your way, using a map). The missing section must identify and give more information about the report.
Question 16: Again there are two key links. The previous paragraph introduces the idea of problems with navigation. The missing section might expand on this. In the following paragraph, the use of the definite article in the phrase *the extra fuel*, suggests that this has been mentioned before.

Answers:
15 E   **16** B

Note these tips for the other questions:

Question 17: The previous section says that navigation problems can lead to *tears or worse* – what would be worse? Look for a paragraph which enlarges on this.
Question 18: Two key links. Look at the beginning of the following paragraph. Find a paragraph which relates to *Her*. To check that you are right, see if the beginning of the missing paragraph links with the last sentence of the paragraph before.
Question 19: The following paragraph begins with direct speech. Look for a paragraph which introduces this. To check your answer, see what the first word refers back to.
Question 20: Be careful, the missing paragraph here relates back to the beginning of the text. (Remember that you should always keep the whole structure of the text in mind.)

▶ Now complete the questions in **Part 2**. When you've finished, you can check your answers on page 47.

Paper 1, Part 3

▶ Turn to **Part 3** on page 26 and follow steps 1–3 in the General Advice for **questions 21** and **22**. Then turn back to this page.

- What is the text about?
- How do most people feel about the topic?
- What answers did you guess for questions 21 and 22?

▶ Now find the information in the text and answer **questions 21** and **22**.

Question 21 – The options

A This may be true, but there's nothing in the text to say so. Stick to the facts in the text.

B The text says good speakers *draw heavily on experience to develop their skills,* another way of saying *go on learning from talks they give.* This is the correct answer.

C The text uses the phrase *natural ease* so you may choose this option if you are reading carelessly. But the meaning is different: good speakers only appear to be at ease because of the techniques they have learned.

D The text says the opposite: good speakers *prepare well.*

Question 22 – The options

A The writer does suggest going on a course but it isn't her main advice.

B This sounds like a good idea but it is not mentioned in the text.

C The text says *there is no substitute for getting out and doing it ... take every opportunity to do so.* This is the correct answer.

D Again, this sounds like a good idea but it is not mentioned in the text.

> **Special points to remember**
> Beware of options which
> - use words from the text but give a different meaning.
> - sound likely but where there's no evidence in the text.

▶ Now complete the questions for **Part 3**. When you have finished, you will find the answers on page 47.

Paper 1, Part 4

▶ Turn to **Part 4** on page 28 and follow the steps in the General Advice to answer the questions.

PAPER 2 WRITING

This paper consists of two parts, with one task of approximately 250 words in each. In **Part 1** there is no choice of topic, while in **Part 2** you will have four topics to choose from. Each question carries equal marks. You have 2 hours to complete the paper.

The types of writing (or *formats*) you may be asked to produce include **formal** and **informal letters**, **reports** and **articles**, as well as shorter pieces like **notes** and **memos**. Usually the question states the format required but sometimes it is less specific. In this case, any suitable format will be acceptable. For example, if you are asked to write an entry for a competition, you could simply begin with an appropriate heading, or you could include the instructions in a letter or note.

It's important to think about the special characteristics of each type of writing and the following notes list some of the main ones:

Letters need an appropriate **salutation** (*Dear Sir/Mr X,*) and **subscription** (*Yours sincerely/faithfully,*) – make sure you know the rules for these. Letters should also have a suitable introduction and conclusion and be divided into clear **paragraphs**. The style depends on whether the letter is formal or informal. Note that in the CAE exam it's not necessary to include the address(es).

Personal notes and **Messages** are even more informal than informal letters and there are no fixed rules about layout. The day, date or time is usually stated at the top; you can use a shortened address or omit the address completely; you can begin with *Dear ...,* with a first name, or just with an initial, depending on your relationship.

Memos are a form of note or message between colleagues in a business context. They usually have a space at the top where the names of the sender and recipient, the date and sometimes the subject are written. The language is generally more formal than in a note to a friend.

Information sheets/Leaflets/Brochures: the layout and organisation need to be designed to catch the reader's attention and present information as clearly as possible. Start with a direct and eye-catching **main heading** and break up the information into short easy-to-read sections with clear **subheadings**. The style should be direct and friendly, so that the reader wants to read on.

Articles need a **headline** to give an idea of the subject and also to catch the reader's attention. They should **begin** and **end** in an interesting way and should be written with the particular age and interests of the readership in mind. For example, if the article is for a college magazine, it should appeal to teenagers.

Reports should have a clear **heading**, an **introduction** and a **conclusion**. The information should be logically organised into separate paragraphs or sections and it's sometimes helpful to give these **subheadings** as well.

Reviews (of books, films or magazines, for example) should begin with an **introduction** or overview of the subject, include detailed comments on successful and unsuccessful features with reasons, and finish with an overall **verdict**, summing up your opinion.

Marking

Each writing task receives two separate marks: a general impression mark and a task specific mark.

1 The **general impression mark scheme** is on a scale of 0–5, with 0 for completely irrelevant or illegible work (or an answer which is fewer than 50 words) and the maximum of 5 for a fully-completed task with a good range of structure and vocabulary and minimal errors.

2 The **task-specific mark scheme** is different for each question, and covers the following areas:

- **Content:** Does your answer cover all the main points mentioned in the question?

- **Organisation and cohesion:** Is the writing clearly and logically organised? Are the ideas well-linked?

- **Range:** Is there a good variety of structures and vocabulary? Is the use of English natural and effective? Is the work free from frequent or serious errors?

- **Register and format:** Are these appropriate for the task and context?

- **Target reader:** Is your answer likely to have the intended effect on the reader?

Other points

Length: The examiner won't count the number of words you've written. You'll only lose marks for a long answer if you've included irrelevant information, or for a short answer if you've left out some important points.

Layout: You are expected to be familiar with the normal layout for a letter, report, etc.

Spelling: You will lose marks for poor spelling if it interferes with communication. American spelling is fine as long as it is used consistently.

Handwriting: If your work is difficult to read, you will also lose marks. If the examiner cannot read it at all, you'll get 0!

General Advice

- Read the **instructions** and the **written texts** very carefully. Underline or circle the important points – you'll lose marks if you don't do everything the question asks you to.
- Think about the **purpose** of the piece of writing, and what **effect** you want it to have on the reader. If you really try to **imagine** yourself in the situation, you will write a better, more convincing answer.
- Make a **plan** of the main points.
- Make sure you use the appropriate **layout** for the type of writing. Consider whether there are any special features of **language** or **style** you should use.
- Keep roughly to the **word limit** – but don't waste time counting every word!
- Leave time to **check** your work carefully afterwards. Don't lose marks because of careless mistakes!

Paper 2, Part 1

The first thing you notice when you look at this section of the paper is how much reading there is to do. This means that you have to deal with written information in some way before you can tackle the writing task. For example, you may have to select the important points from one or more texts, summarise the information or find the differences between two texts. In other words, Part 1 tests effective **reading** as well as writing.

The second important point is that you may be asked to produce more than one piece of writing – a letter **and** a brief note, for example. Make sure you do **all** the parts of the question – if you leave out one part, even if it's a very short part, you may lose half the possible marks or more.

Now let's look at Part 1 in Test 1.

▶ Turn to **question 1** on page 30 and read the instructions and the letter to Pat.

1 Completeness and Relevance

Which of the points below would it be important to mention in the letter of complaint? Which would be irrelevant? Why?

- ☐ It was Tony's birthday.
- ☐ The kitchen was warm.
- ☐ You discussed the choice of restaurant.
- ☐ The steak was tough.
- ☐ You saw an advert for the restaurant.
- ☐ The peas were tinned.
- ☐ The restaurant was empty.
- ☐ Tony had a vegetarian dish.
- ☐ It was freezing.
- ☐ Tony's food was lukewarm.
- ☐ The menu looked promising.
- ☐ The bill was enormous.
- ☐ There was no lobster.
- ☐ There was a charge for bread.
- ☐ The waiter was scruffy and off-hand.
- ☐ There was a service charge.

What **other** information would you need to give? Feel free to invent extra details like dates and times, but don't change any of the information given.

▶ Look at the advertisement and the restaurant bill, and underline or circle any points which support your complaint and should be mentioned in the letter.

2 Planning

This is an essential stage – not an additional extra! It's the time when you decide how to organise what you want to say so that your message is as clear and effective as possible. You will need an **introduction** stating the reason for writing and then **separate paragraphs** giving details of the various problems. Your **conclusion** should say exactly what you expect the restaurant to do.

3 Layout/Language/Style

As this is a formal letter, remember how and where to put the date, salutation and subscription. Divide the letter into paragraphs by indenting (beginning a short distance inside the margin). Remember suitable phrases for this sort of letter (*I am writing to complain about ... I must insist that you ...*)

Special point to remember
It's not a good idea to 'lift' phrases or whole sentences from the texts to use in your writing. They will probably sound wrong because the style or register is inappropriate and you will lose marks as a result. Try to express the same ideas in your own words.

Paper 2, Part 2

Take time to read all the questions and decide on the question you can answer best. This may not be the one that looks easiest at first glance. Make sure you know what is required in each case: Do you understand the **situation**, can you imagine yourself in it? Do you know the necessary **vocabulary** and **structures**? Do you know how to **organise** and **lay out** that type of writing?

When you've decided on a question, read the instructions very carefully and underline or circle the key points. Many students lose marks in the exam because they leave out one or more important points. Remember, **every** word in the instructions counts!

▶ Turn to **Part 2** on page 32 and read the instructions for **questions 2–5**. Look to see what **type** of writing is required in each case, what style or register would be appropriate and what special vocabulary or structure you might need.

Question 2

You are asked to write a **report** (see notes on page 10), which is the clearest way of presenting the information that the family needs. You can assume that you would send it with a brief covering note, so don't worry about addressing the family or including any pleasantries. First decide on your main heading (which should be easy!) and subheadings.

The writer asks for information about the education system in your country but this doesn't call for a long, detailed survey. The emphasis should be on giving the basic facts clearly and keeping to points which are relevant to the writer. If you happen to know something about the English educational system, you could mention any differences, but this isn't necessary to produce a good answer.

The second part of the question asks for practical suggestions. It's probably easiest to mention real schools that you know but if you have to invent schools, that's fine too.

Question 3

This requires an **article** (see notes on page 10) for an international students' magazine, so think about the likely age and interests of the readers before you start – a touch of humour will probably be helpful. The question calls for some narrative (how your hobby started), some explanation (what appeals to you about your hobby), some information (where you go to add to your collection), and some description (a particular item you have or would like to have).

If your hobby is rather unusual, you will probably need to explain exactly what it involves first of all. If it's quite a common hobby, it may be more difficult to write about interestingly unless you have some special stories to tell. In either case, the important thing is to convey your interest and enthusiasm.

Don't forget to think of a suitable heading and to start and finish the article in an interesting way – imagine you very much want your article to be accepted for publication!

Question 4

The question asks for a **proposal** but doesn't specify a particular format. You could write your answer as a long memo, borrowing the headings from the memo in the question, or as a letter. Whichever approach you adopt, the style should be quite formal.

The first part of the task really calls for a kind of **review** (see notes on page 10) but with the emphasis on the positive features. Bear in mind, too, that the items you recommend are for an educational institution so you should be able to argue that they will be useful for, or of interest to, a wide range of students. (Remember that you need to suggest two or more items.)

For the second part of the task, try to think of libraries you know and problems you have experienced, e.g. having to queue, not having anywhere to sit, difficulties with the cataloguing system, etc. Explain the problem(s) and suggest clear, practical solutions. The main aim is obviously to make your proposal so convincing that the librarian cannot help but take up your suggestions.

Question 5

Here you need to write an **informal letter** (see notes on page 9) but one which is to be sent to a number of friends rather than just one. It's not usual to write *Dear Friend* in English, so leave a space after *Dear* – or put *Dear (name of friend)* – as if you were going to fill each person's name in afterwards.

A good answer will mention particular problems with the decoration (e.g. peeling wallpaper, flaking or discoloured paint, etc.) so if you don't have the necessary vocabulary, it's probably best to avoid this question. If you do attempt it, take a few moments to write down all the words and phrases to do with the topic that you know. It's very annoying to realise later that you forgot to include some really good specialised vocabulary!

The other important part of the question is to make your party sound so appealing that none of your friends will want to miss it!

PAPER 3 ENGLISH IN USE

Paper 3 is divided into six parts with about 75–80 questions in total. You have 1 hour 30 minutes in which to complete it.

This part of the exam tests your knowledge of different aspects of the language system. These include **grammar**, **vocabulary**, **spelling** and **punctuation**, as you would expect, and also **register** (choosing appropriate words and expressions for formal and informal contexts), and **cohesion** and **coherence** (using language to link different parts of a text, or different ideas, together).

Each correct answer in the six parts of Paper 3 is given one mark.

> **Tip**
> ▮ When you're working through Paper 3 in the practice tests, time yourself to see which parts take you the longest. Then when you take the exam, plan your time carefully so you allow enough time for each of the sections.

Paper 3, Parts 1 and 2

This section consists of two blank-filling (or 'cloze') exercises with 15 blanks to fill in each. The first focuses mainly on **vocabulary** and there are multiple choice answers to choose from. The second focuses mainly on **structural points**, prepositions, articles, verb forms and so on, and there are no multiple choice answers.

> **General Advice**
> • Read through the whole text before you think about possible answers – ask yourself what it's about and what the writer's purpose is.
> • Notice the style – is it formal or fairly informal? The words you choose will have to fit in with this style.
> • Make sure the answers you give fit logically **and** grammatically.

Paper 3, Part 1 Multiple choice cloze

▶ Turn to *Save money on the book that aims to save animals* on page 34 and read the text quickly without worrying about the gaps. Think about the general meaning, the writer's purpose and the style. Then read the first paragraph again more carefully, looking particularly at **questions 5–7**.

When you look at the possible answers, you will need to consider various points.

1 Does the word fit logically?
2 Does the word fit grammatically?
3 Is it **exactly** the right word for the context?

In **questions 5** and **6**, the answers are linked. Looking at the options for **question 5** first, we need a verb which can be followed by an object (*animals*) and an infinitive without *to*. This eliminates **A** *enable* and **C** *allow*, which are followed by a verb with *to*. **D** *assist* is also unsuitable as it is usually followed by the preposition *in* or *with*. The correct answer is **B** *help* which can be followed by a verb with or without *to*.

In **question 6**, we find two pairs of words which look similar and which are in the same general area of meaning. We are looking for an intransitive verb (one which doesn't take an object) so we can eliminate **A** *preserve* (you preserve food, for example) and **B** *conserve* (you might conserve your energy). **C** *revive* means to become active again and this doesn't fit the context. Only answer **D** *survive* is suitable.

In **question 7**, the sentence refers to *terrible results* – so do you expect a positive or negative word to fill the gap? Options **B** *interest*, **C** *care* and **D** *concern* are all fairly positive words and they don't fit the context. In addition, when we look at the grammar, we can eliminate **B** *interest* because it is followed by the preposition *in*, not *for* as in the text. The only answer which fits logically **and** grammatically is **A** *greed*.

▶ Now do the rest of the task. When you've finished, you can check your answers on page 47.

Paper 3, Part 2 Structural cloze

▶ Turn to *Olympic Gold* on page 36 and read the text quickly without worrying about the gaps. Again think about the general meaning, the writer's purpose and the style. Then read the first paragraph more carefully, thinking particularly about the answers to **questions 16/17** and **21/22**.

It's important to think about the **kind** of word which is needed in each space. Don't make an elementary mistake by putting in something which doesn't fit grammatically at all. It's usually easy to spot a missing article or a preposition but it may be harder to know when a verb or a linking word is needed. So remember to look at the **whole** sentence, not just the words before or after the space, and to look for any clues which may help.

When you read the first sentence of the text, you find that it is in two main parts, linked by the word in **question 16**. So this must be a linking word concerning time.

If you only look at the word after **question 17**, *place*, you might think you need an article or perhaps a preposition. In fact, when you look at the whole sentence, you find you need an *-ing* form verb (... *there was something ...ing*). The general meaning must be 'happening' but the verb has to combine with the word *place*.

The answers are **16** *when* and **17** *taking*.

Now look at **question 21**. Here another linking word is needed – this time to connect two contrasting ideas: he was only of modest standard + he won the gold medal. The answer is *Although*.

Sometimes an important clue is slightly hidden. The clue for **question 22** is *teamed up* but it comes earlier in the sentence. You team up *with* a person, so this is the correct answer.

> **Points to remember**
> - Correct spelling is essential – take care when you fill in the answer sheet.
> - You'll lose marks if you write more than **one** word in each space.

▶ Now do the rest of the task. When you've finished, you can check your answers on page 47.

Paper 3, Part 3 Error correction

In this exercise, you have to **recognise** and **correct errors** in a piece of writing, which will involve either:

- identifying unnecessary words **or**
- correcting spelling and/or punctuation errors.

This is a very useful kind of task which practises the skills you need when you have to check your own or someone else's work.

The instructions tell you to indicate the correct lines with a tick (✓). You can expect a maximum of 5 correct lines in the text.

> **General Advice**
> - Read the instructions very carefully. What you need to do varies according to the kind of mistake you're correcting.
> - Read the text quickly to get the general picture.

> - Read it again much more carefully, line by line. It's easy to miss a mistake if you're thinking mainly about the meaning.
> - When you've made all the corrections you can, read through the piece again to make sure it makes sense.

Let's look at this task in Test 1.

▶ Turn to *The Big Sleep* on page 37 and read the instructions. Next read the text quickly, without worrying about any mistakes, to find out what it's about. Finally look very carefully at the first part of the text and answer **questions 31–35**.

The first example sentence (**0**) illustrates a typical type of error – the use of an article where one isn't needed. There's another error like this later in the text.

In line **31** the expression *builds out* probably looks unfamiliar to you – this is because it doesn't exist! We say *build* or possibly *build up*, so *out* is the unnecessary word.

In line **32**, there's an unnecessary preposition. The verb *help* is followed by an object (*skin cells*) and a verb with or without *to* (*to regenerate*), as we saw in the first cloze exercise. The preposition *with* is unnecessary.

In line **33**, the phrase *do we really need* looks right at first glance. But when we look at the **whole** sentence, we find there's no need for the auxiliary *do*.

You shouldn't have found any errors in line **34** because there aren't any! But don't forget to put a tick in the space. In line **35**, the phrase *in asleep* should look a bit strange. This is because *in* is a preposition and should be followed by a noun, not an adjective like *asleep*. The unnecessary word is *in*.

> **Points to remember: Correcting unnecessary words**
> In this type of exercise, look especially carefully at:
> - definite and indefinite articles (*a/the*): think about the rules for using them.
> - auxiliary verbs (*be/do/have*): check that they have been used correctly.
> - relative pronouns (*which/that/who*, etc.): check that these are not used unnecessarily.
> - any expressions you haven't seen before: they may not be correct.

▶ Now do the rest of this task. When you've finished, you can check your answers on page 47.

Paper 3, Part 4 Word formation

In this task, you have to fill in gaps in two short texts using the correct forms of prompt words given.

The words you need will be a variety of parts of speech including nouns, verbs, adjectives and adverbs. To form them you may need to make any of the following changes to the prompt word:

add a **prefix** (like *un-* or *in-*) e.g. *active – inactive* (adj)
add a **suffix** (like *-ly* or *-ness*) e.g. *willing – willingly* (adv); *willingness* (n)
make a **spelling change**, e.g. *wide – width* (n); *half – halve* (v)
combine two words to make a **compound**, e.g. *head – big-headed* (adj); *headline* (n)

General Advice
- Read through each text first, so that you know what it's about.
- Look carefully at each gap and decide what **kind** of word (noun, verb, etc.) is needed. Think about the change which is needed to form the new word.
- Make sure the word fits correctly. It may need to be made negative or plural.
- When you've finished, read through the text inserting the new words to check that it makes sense.

▶ Turn to page 38 and read the instructions. Next read the first text quickly, without worrying about the gaps, to find out what it's about. Then answer **questions 47–53**.

The word needed for **question 47** is linked by *and* with the noun *age*, so you know that you need to form a noun from *able*.
Question 48: Reading the whole sentence, you can guess that golf is different from other sports. You need to make the preposition *like* negative.
Question 49: Notice that *alert*, the word following the gap, is an adjective. The missing word must be an adverb qualifying *alert*.
Question 51: Be careful here. What kind of word is needed to qualify *good*? (See **question 49** above.)
Question 52: The word needed here is an adjective meaning 'higher' or 'towards the top'. (What is the opposite?)
Question 53: You need to add a suffix here to form a noun. Be careful about the spelling!

The answers are **47** *ability*, **48** *Unlike*, **49** *mentally* **50** *rotation*, **51** *reasonably*, **52** *upper*, **53** *endurance*

Points to remember: Word formation
- Sometimes you can form more than one word which fits grammatically. For example, if the prompt word is *care*, the adjective could be *careful* or *careless*. Make sure you choose the one which is logical in the context.
- You may have to make more than one change so the word fits the meaning. For example, you may have to add *-ly* to form an adjective and also a prefix like *un-* to make the word negative, e.g. **un***fortunately*.

▶ Now read the second text and answer **questions 54–61**. When you've finished, you can check your answers on page 47.

Paper 3, Part 5 Register cloze

In this task, you have to **transfer information** from a text in **one register** (e.g. formal) to a text in **another register** (e.g. informal) by filling gaps in the second text. This is a test of your ability to write in different styles and to recognise which words and expressions are appropriate in different contexts.

The choice of language depends on the **relationship** between the writer and reader (Do they know each other well? Is it a fairly formal relationship?), on the **subject** (Is it serious or not very important?), and also on the **situation** (Is it necessary to be tactful, persuasive, forceful, etc.?). For example, the following are all ways of asking for information but they are suitable for very different contexts:

I should be grateful if you would send me details of the post you are advertising.
I really must insist that you provide a full explanation for your actions.
Could you let me know your thoughts on the matter when you get a minute?

General Advice
- Read the first text very carefully. Notice not only the information but also the **context** for the second piece of writing.
- Read the second text very carefully. Notice the style and study the example.
- Remember you can use one or two words (but no more) and you can't use words which appear in the first text.
- Make sure you give exactly the same information and that the language fits grammatically **and** stylistically.

▶ Turn to **Part 5** on page 39 and read the booking conditions. Don't worry about words you don't know for the moment. Next read the informal note and notice the style. Then look at **questions 62–67**.

- What examples of formal language can you find in the first text?
- What do you think the relationship between the writer and the reader is?
- What examples of informal language can you find in the second text?

In the example (**0**), notice how the passive structure *Reservations should be made ...* becomes *We have to arrange things ... .* For **question 62**, we need an expression which means the same as *14 days*. It must be a noun because there's an article before it. The answer is *fortnight*.
For **questions 63** and **64**, we have to find another way of expressing *subject to the availability of accommodation and flights*. For **question 64**, we know we need a verb to follow *can* and that the meaning is 'obtain'. The verb must also combine with *us*, which follows. The answers are *depends (on)* and *find* or *get*.
For **questions 65–67**, we again need to express a formal sentence more simply. Instead of *We suggest that*, we must find an adjective to follow *It's ... .* For *full payment*, we need a noun meaning 'quantity' to follow *whole*. For *preparation of travel documents*, we need an adjective to go with *get (things) ... .* The answers are *advisable, amount* and *ready*.

▶ Now do the rest of this task. When you've finished, you can check your answers on page 47.

Paper 3, Part 6 Discourse cloze

In this task you have to choose the best phrase or sentence to fill gaps in a text. Like the paragraph cloze exercise in Paper 1, this tests your understanding of the way **the text is organised** and the way **the writer develops the argument**. Here the missing parts are shorter – just a phrase or sentence.

General Advice
- Read through the incomplete text first and make sure you understand what the argument or sequence of events is.
- Think about what **might** be missing at each gap before you look at the possible answers. You might not be able to guess, but the thought process will make it easier to choose the right answer.
- Check that your answer fits the space grammatically **and** logically.

▶ Turn to *Migraine Headaches* on page 40 and read through the text quickly for the general meaning. Then read it again more carefully, thinking particularly about **questions 75** and **76**.

It's important to notice that in the first paragraph the writer is talking about *ordinary* headaches, while *migraine* headaches are discussed in the rest of the text. So, for **question 75**, we need a sentence which makes this distinction and links the two paragraphs.

The second paragraph describes the main characteristics of migraine headaches compared to ordinary headaches, so **question 76** should mention one of these differences which also relates to the sentence which follows.

The answers are **E** and **H**.

Notice clues for the other questions:
77 The sentence before describes how migraine attacks vary from person to person. Is this the only variation?
78 The two sentences which follow talk about the danger of doing certain things *in excess*. Look for a sentence which mentions this idea of excess.
79 The sentence before says that not having enough food can be harmful. Is this the only thing the body needs?
80 The text has mentioned things we do which can cause migraine attacks and the sentence before advises us to stop doing them.

▶ Now do the rest of this task. When you've finished, you can check your answers on page 47.

PAPER 4 LISTENING

The Listening paper is divided into four parts with 30–40 questions in total and it takes about 45 minutes. Here are a few general points:

The instructions for the questions are spoken on the tape as well as printed on the exam paper. The recordings in **Parts 1, 3** and **4** are played twice but in **Part 2** the piece is played only once.

The voices you hear will speak standard English but there may be a variety of British and non-British accents. A few of the recordings used are authentic – in other words, recordings of real conversations rather than actors reading a script. This book provides practice in listening to authentic material and different accents, as do most coursebooks, so you should be well-prepared for this.

Your answers need to be correctly spelt!

At the end of the test, you have to transfer your answers on to the special answer sheet and there is time allowed for this. **Be careful**, it's easy to make mistakes.

- Make sure your answers match the questions – if you overlook one answer, all the rest will be numbered wrongly.
- Check for spelling or grammar mistakes which would lose you marks.
- Don't change your original answer by adding more details or abbreviating it.

General Advice
- Always read the instructions carefully, even if you think you know what to do. There may be small variations in questions from exam to exam.
- Study the task. If it's a table, look at the headings and the way it's laid out. If it's sentences, read them carefully. Think about the vocabulary.
- Study the questions so you know exactly what information you have to listen for. If you think about the questions and try to predict the answers where possible, it will make the listening task easier.

Paper 4, Parts 1 and 2

The recordings for **Parts 1** and **2** are fairly short (about 2 minutes each) and are usually monologues. The questions test your understanding of specific information in the recordings and you will have to fill in missing information in notes or sentences.

Let's look at **Part 1** in Test 1. Turn to page 41 and follow these steps.

1 Read the instructions very carefully. Make sure you know exactly what you have to do.
2 Study the table. Look at the headings so you understand how the table is organised and what you need to fill in. Think about the words in the table.
3 Study the questions. Try to predict some of the missing information. Can you suggest answers for **questions 1** and **3**? Notice that the table is filled in in note form (without all the articles and prepositions) so your answers can be in note form too.

Now play the tape **twice** and answer the questions. When you've finished, you can check your answers on page 47.

Now turn to **Part 2** on page 42 and follow these steps.

1 Read carefully through the instructions and the text.
2 Think about the missing information. Are there any answers you can guess? For **question 13**, for example, what could a parent or teacher be asked for in order to prove that the child did the work without any help?
3 Remember, **Part 2** is played **once only** so it's obviously important to listen very carefully.

Special point to remember
- Sometimes the information in the recording uses slightly different words from those in the question. Be ready for this. For example, in **question 12**, *Entries should be no longer than ...* is expressed as *the maximum length for each entry ... .* There is also a change of wording in **question 17**.

Now play the tape **once** and answer the questions. When you've finished, you can check your answers on page 47.

Paper 4, Part 3

Part 3 is longer than the other sections (about 4 minutes) and is usually a dialogue or an interview. The questions test your understanding of the text as a whole, including the speaker's **attitude**, as well as specific information you hear. You may have to complete a set of notes or answer multiple choice questions.

With note-completion, marks are awarded for the correct **key word(s)** so there is no need to write a full, grammatically complete sentence. There is only enough space on the answer sheet for about three words and if you try to write more, you'll simply be wasting time.

Turn to **Part 3** on page 43 and follow these steps.

1 Read the instructions and the text.
2 Try to predict answers – for example **questions 18, 19** and **25**.

Special point to remember
• Make sure your answer fits grammatically. For example, in **question 18**, the answer needs to be a gerund (like *travelling*). Similarly, in **questions 25** and **29**, *to* must be followed by an infinitive.

Now play the tape **twice** and answer the questions. When you've finished, you can check your answers on page 47.

Paper 4, Part 4

Part 4 consists of a number of short extracts (about 30 seconds each) with pauses between them. You may be asked to identify things like the **context** (the situation where people are speaking), the **topic** they are talking about, or the **function** (whether they are apologising, complaining and so on).

Turn to **Part 4** on page 44 and follow these steps.

1 Read the general instructions and the instructions for Task One.
2 Look at each item in the list, and think about how it is used.
3 Read the instructions for Task Two and the list of reasons.
4 Be prepared for the information to be given in slightly different words from the question.

Special point to remember
• Sometimes the precise answer isn't stated and you have to use clues in the recording to work out what the answer is. Listen carefully for the clues. In Task One, for example, the clues to **question 32** are in *bodywork*, *interior* and *tyres*. Can you find the clues for the other questions?

Now play the tape **twice** and answer the questions. When you've finished, you can check your answers on page 47.

PAPER 5 SPEAKING

In the interview, you will be examined with another candidate and there will be two examiners. One examiner, known as the **interlocutor**, will work with you, explaining the tasks and helping with any problems, as well as assessing your English. The other examiner, known as the **assessor**, will concentrate on assessing your English. The whole interview lasts about 15 minutes and there are four parts which are designed to test different speaking skills.

Most people find it less stressful to be examined with another candidate and if you are in a pair with a friend, it will probably help you to feel more relaxed. If you haven't met your partner before, however, don't worry. Working with someone you don't know can have advantages too – it may be easier to think of genuine questions to ask and more natural for you to exchange information.

Here is a summary of what happens in each of the four parts.

Part 1 (About 3 minutes) In this phase the examiners will introduce themselves, and you and your partner will be expected to introduce yourselves (or each other), to take part in a relaxed conversation and to talk about your backgrounds, interests, career plans and so on. This phase tests your **general interactional and social English**.

Part 2 (3 or 4 minutes) You will be given pictures to describe and comment on, and each candidate will have a chance to talk for about a minute. This phase tests your ability to **organise your ideas** and **express yourself clearly** and **coherently**.

Part 3 (3 or 4 minutes) You will have to solve a problem or reach a decision about something by discussing the matter with your partner. This type of activity is designed to test your ability to **give and invite opinions** and **reasons**, and to **negotiate a decision** with your partner.

Part 4 (3 or 4 minutes) In this phase, you have to report to the examiner the decision you reached in Part 3 and also take part in a more general discussion about the topic. This phase tests your ability to **report, summarise** and **explain** clearly, and to **develop a discussion**.

Marking

In the Speaking paper, you are assessed on your performance in the test as a whole, not on individual parts. Each examiner awards separate marks.

The assessor awards marks for each of the following criteria:

- **Grammar and Vocabulary:** using a good range of structures and vocabulary accurately and appropriately.
- **Discourse Management:** expressing ideas and opinions clearly and coherently, and without too much hesitation.
- **Pronunciation:** being easy to understand and using English pronunciation features (sounds, stress, intonation) reasonably accurately.
- **Interactive Communication:** playing a full and effective part in the discussions with your partner and with the examiners.

The interlocutor awards one global mark.

General Advice
- Listen very carefully! The instructions aren't written down, so you need to understand and remember them.
- Don't be afraid to ask the **examiner** to repeat something you haven't heard or to clarify something you haven't understood. This is much better than losing marks because you haven't done what you were asked to do!
- Remember that you are expected to co-operate with your **partner**. You will lose marks if you try to do all the talking or if you don't listen and respond to what your partner says.
- Don't be afraid to ask your **partner** to repeat or clarify something you haven't understood. You will be assessed on your individual performance and you won't lose marks if you have difficulty in understanding your partner.

Let's look at the four parts of the Speaking paper in more detail.

Paper 5, Part 1

In this phase, the examiners will introduce themselves to you and you will be expected to introduce yourself or maybe to introduce your partner, if you know them. Here is some useful language:

Responding to the examiners:	Introducing your partner:
How do you do?	*May I introduce my friend/partner ...*
You reply:	*He/She comes from ....*
How do you do?	*We're both studying in the same school.*
I'm .../My name is ...	*We've known each other for ...*
You reply:	*Actually we've just met!*
I'm pleased to meet you.	
Introducing yourself:	
My name is .../I'm .... and I come from ...	

As the conversation develops, you should be prepared to answer questions (or ask your partner) about such general topics as:

- your family
- the place you live
- how you travel to work/school/college
- your interests and hobbies
- why you're learning English
- your plans for the future

If you're studying in Britain, you may also be asked specific questions about the main differences compared with your own country, or about aspects of British life that you especially like or dislike.

The examiner may suggest that you ask your partner a question. If so, try to put the question into **your own words** so that it sounds as natural and conversational as possible. Remember, too, that this is an **advanced level** examination. Try to go beyond the level of boring 'small talk' and introduce some really interesting points into the conversation! Listen carefully to your partner and show interest in what they say.

▶ Turn to page 45 and look at the questions in **Part 1** of Test 1. Think about the answers you would give and also how you could ask your partner for information as naturally as possible.

Tip

■ If you're going to do the interview with someone you know, it's not a good idea to prepare together for Part 1 or to learn short dialogues by heart. It's always obvious to examiners if you've rehearsed beforehand and you'll get more marks for spontaneous communication.

Paper 5, Part 2

In this phase, you will each have the chance to describe and make comments on one or more pictures.

For each task, one candidate is expected to speak for about one minute without interruption. It's not meant to be a question and answer session so, while your partner is talking about a picture, you should listen very carefully and think about what's being said. When your partner has finished, you will be asked to comment briefly (for about 20 seconds), saying whether you agree or disagree with what your partner has said, or whether you want to add any points which haven't been mentioned, for example.

The important thing with Part 2 is to try to do more than simply describe what you can see in the picture(s). If you talk about your **personal reaction** to what you see, you'll be able to use a wider range of language and you should earn more marks.

There are various types of picture prompt and task. Here are some typical examples:

Describe and contrast (two similar pictures) – comment on the main differences between the pictures.
Describe, hypothesise and comment (two different pictures but with a common theme) – suggest what the two pictures have in common.
Describe and comment (each candidate has the same set of 5–8 pictures on a related theme) – Candidate A describes two pictures; Candidate B then comments on them.
Describe and identify (each candidate has the same set of 5–8 pictures but in a different order) – Candidate A describes two pictures; Candidate B has to identify them. There are also variations on this task where Candidate B has an extra picture or one different picture which they must identify and describe.

▶ Turn to page 45 and follow the instructions for Tasks 1 and 2 in **Part 2** of Test 1.

After you finish **Task 1**, compare the pictures carefully again and discuss how you could have improved your performance. What else could you have said to describe the pictures better? What vocabulary could you have used? Ask your teacher for any words or expressions you didn't know and make a careful note of them. (You may be interested to know that the pictures show the same family group photographed in 1971 and then in 1989.)

After you finish **Task 2**, study the pictures and discuss your performance again. Make a note of useful vocabulary.

Tip

■ Don't worry if you can't think of the **exact** word for something. This happens to everybody sometimes! You won't be expected to know very specialised vocabulary and you won't lose marks if you use another suitable word or find an alternative way of expressing what you want to say.

■ Try not to end negatively by saying something like 'Sorry, that's all I can think of!'.

Paper 5, Part 3

In this phase, you will work with your partner to solve a problem or reach a decision about something. This task is intended to give you the opportunity to express your own opinions and also respond to your partner's views. In other words, it should be a discussion rather than an argument, and the emphasis should be on **co-operation** and **negotiation** rather than winning or losing! Aim for a balance where each person has an equal amount of time to express their views and where you really listen to each other. Useful language to practise would include:

---

asking about and expressing **opinions**
asking about and giving **reasons** for opinions
asking for and making **suggestions**
persuading
expressing strong **agreement**, mild **disagreement**, etc.

You should discuss your ideas fully and try to reach agreement but if you have to agree to disagree in the end, that's alright too. You will be marked on how well you tackle the task and on the language you use, not on the results you reach.

Here are some typical tasks:

Interpret and discuss (Cartoon) – decide what point the cartoonist is trying to make, say whether you agree or disagree.
Evaluate and select (Set of pictures representing places, activities, objects, etc.) – choose the ones which would be most appropriate for a particular purpose. In **Evaluate and rank order** tasks, put the items in order of merit (e.g. 1 for the most suitable, 2 for the next, etc.).

Exchange opinions (Picture(s)/cartoon/diagram) – talk about a topic; plan a party; suggest suitable subjects for a radio programme, etc.

▶ Turn to page 46 and follow the instructions for **Part 3** of Test 1.

Tip

■ It's important to keep the conversation going by using expressions like *Now, let me see* ... or *Let's just think about* ... , called 'fillers', which give you time to think, and it's a good idea to practise these.

■ When you practise for Part 3, it's a good idea to record your conversation if possible. Listen to the recording afterwards to see how balanced the discussion was and how wide a range of language you used. If there isn't a tape recorder available, you could ask another student to listen to your discussion and comment on these points.

Paper 5, Part 4

In this phase, you tell the examiner about your discussion in the previous phase and report any decisions you reached, together with your reasons. It's a good idea to practise this part of the interview too because you'll need to be able to **summarise**, using reported speech, and **explain** clearly.

You will usually be asked a few more questions related to the same topic. If there aren't any more questions, don't worry, it's probably because the examiner has already heard enough to make a clear assessment.

Finally, don't forget to thank the examiners and say goodbye!

Practice Test 1
Paper 1 – Reading
Part 1

Answer questions **1–14** by referring to the newspaper article about taking children on long-distance flights on page **23**.

For questions **1–14**, answer by choosing from the list (**A–H**) on the right below. Some of the choices may be required more than once.

Note: When more than one answer is required, these may be given **in any order**.

Which section mentions

children's clothes?	1 ...E.....	**A** Book your seats in advance
a road accident?	2 ...H...	
features of airline seats?	3 ...B...	**B** Fly economy class
airline food?	4 A.......	
sleeping arrangements?	5 ..G....	**C** Stop worrying, relax
other passengers?	6 ..D..... 7 ....B...	**D** Make friends
examples of children being difficult?	8 ....C 9 ......F	**E** Be flexible
a delayed flight?	10 ..H......	**F** Use the flight attendant
the high cost of business class?	11 ...B....	**G** Make yourself comfortable
extra equipment to take with you?	12 ....G...	**H** For heaven's sake, go
things for children to play with?	13 ..A...... 14 C	

Look, daddy, I can fly

Long-haul journeys with children can be made bearable if you are well-prepared, David Thomas writes.

The following tips are the fruits of my recent experience of travelling with children who had never flown before, and the experts' advice.

A Book your seats in advance

The key to successful family flying is to ensure that you have a row of seats entirely to yourselves, so that you can spread out and scatter toys without fear of inconveniencing other passengers. Most airlines are fairly co-operative when it comes to dealing with children, but you must arrange things well in advance.

While you are reserving your seats, arrange for special meals for the children. Given any relevant information about allergies or dietary needs, most airlines will supply basic food that stands more chance of being consumed by choosy children than the normal meals served. They may also serve children before the main meal is handed out.

B Fly economy class

For anyone used to the comforts of Club Class, holiday offers that allow business class travel for a small extra payment may seem tempting. There are, however, two arguments against them.

The first is that while the seats in business class are incomparably more comfortable than those in economy, they tend to have fixed armrests. In economy, armrests can be raised, which comes in handy.

Secondly, your fellow passengers are likely to feel far less well-disposed to disruptive young kids if they have just paid a fortune for a little comfort. In economy, the whole place is already half-way to being a cattle truck, so youthful disruption is far less noticeable.

C Stop worrying, relax

No matter how well-behaved a child may be, and no matter how generously supplied with toys, no little boy or girl can sit still and silent through a transatlantic flight. As the children charge up and down the aisle, parents usually follow, apologising as they go, like neurotic cowboys, riding off to round up their runaway calves. The children become resentful, stubborn and, most crucial of all, loud. The row that ensues causes far more disturbance than the children alone could ever have done.

The moral is, let your children have a bit of a runaround. With any luck they will not do anything too drastic. But just in case they do ...

D Make friends

As early as possible in the flight, introduce yourself and your children to the occupants of neighbouring rows. Assure everyone that if they feel disturbed by the children, they only have to mention it to you and action will be taken immediately. This will put you on the side of the angels and will also ensure that nobody dares to say anything.

E Be flexible

The aim, remember is for the children to be as happy as possible for the duration of the flight. So be ruthless in pursuit of this aim. If your son believes that his Batman costume is the ultimate in travel-wear, do not object. You may feel embarrassed being accompanied by a tiny version of the Dark Knight of Gotham City, but he will be happy.

F Use the flight attendant

No matter how perfect your preparations, there will be moments in a long flight when danger threatens. In our case this happened when our two-year old adamantly refused to be seat-belted when required. Luckily, the attendant was able to exert her authority where ours had failed. Something about her uniform, her manner and her air of power seemed to do the trick. So, if in doubt, press the panic button and leave it to the experts.

G Make yourself comfortable

This is the key to everything. The four-seat row in the middle of a 747 is wide enough to allow two small children to sleep on the floor (except at take-off and landing, or when seat belts should be worn), but the floor, naturally enough, is hard. Airline pillows are insufficient to cope with the problem, but if you take an extra small pillow for each child, it should do the trick. This will allow parents to stretch out across the whole row of seats, giving them more room than they would have had in Club Class.

H For heaven's sake, go

No matter how hellish your journey may be – and ours was not helped by a three-hour delay on the tarmac at Gatwick airport, followed by a taxi ride at the far end during which the driver ran over a cow – it is amazing how soon all is forgotten once you get to your destination. This is truly a case in which the end justifies the means. So if you are thinking of taking the family long distance, do not hesitate. Just go.

From *The Times*

Part 2

For questions **15–20**, you must choose which of the paragraphs **A–G** on page **25** fit into the numbered gaps in the following newspaper article. There is one extra paragraph which does not fit in any of the gaps.

The Cost of Getting Lost

Joe Warwick on the A–Z of gender battles

As I studied the London A–Z street guide on the way to a party we were late for, I decided to tell my girlfriend about a new report I had read which said that men were much better map-readers than women. 'Was the report by any chance written by a man?' she asked. 'Yes,' I replied. 'But that's irrelevant. It has been scientifically proven that on average ...' She had stopped listening.

15 E

The reason for the apparent male superiority in navigating could be nature – the interaction between hormones and brain development during the foetal period – or nurture – the different travel experiences available to males as they grow up, with males being given more opportunities to travel by themselves. Either way, there is little doubt that one of the major causes of in-car arguments is disagreement over navigation.

16 D

While the extra fuel puts an unnecessary strain on our wallets and the environment, 'map-rage', as it is becoming known, can put an even greater strain on our relationships. The stress of navigating along an unfamiliar route, combined with the different ways in which men and women communicate and navigate, can lead to tears or worse.

17 G

Although some men may see it as their evolutionary destiny to be the hunter-gatherer / driver-map-reader, it is not always possible in a car. According to the AA report, 79 per cent of women report that if they and their partner are together in the car during the day, their partner will drive. Thus, unwillingly, women are often forced to do the map-reading.

18 F

Her husband Jonathon, a journalist, confesses to the male stereotype of refusing to stop and ask the way: 'I won't ask directions because I don't see the point. I can't stand people giving directions over the phone; just give me the address and I'll find it. We tend to sit down together before we get in the car and go through the route.'

19 A

'We had to go to Fife in Scotland – I can't drive so I was in the passenger seat. And unfortunately I get car sick so I can't read the map. Fife is lovely but finding your way around is pretty complicated. At one point we were driving round in circles.' 'I could have killed him,' confesses Gill. 'The car sickness was just an excuse for doing absolutely nothing. We were travelling in this tiny VW Polo on a boiling hot day, with him complaining because he's got to read the map. It was like having a small child on the seat next to me. We didn't talk for six months after that.'

20 C

'If you'd let me finish, I was going to say that it also says that a minority of women have superior navigation skills to a significant minority of men,' I replied. Significantly, I was, at the same time thinking that neither of us was a member of the respective minorities and that some fool had numbered the houses atrociously.

A Neither takes their navigation disagreements very seriously, but many motoring couples are less relaxed. Andrew Meehan and his then partner Gill Mills, who both work in television, made one car trip too many, as he explains.

B It's estimated that 5 per cent of car journeys are made in unfamiliar areas. A fifth of our mileage during these journeys is the result of navigational mistakes, which means we waste more than 100 million gallons of petrol a year.

C Meanwhile, on the way to the party, I did find the right road eventually but I had to loop round it twice before I found the right house. My girlfriend spent the wasted time smiling sweetly. 'That report is obviously absolutely accurate,' she observed irritatingly.

D Matthew Joint, co-author of the report, is aware of the fiery response from women to his findings: 'I won't tell you what my mother said, and I must say that I'm still fairly wary about discussing my work because I know what an emotive issue it is,' he says.

E The AA-commissioned report, *Psychological Aspects of Navigation*, considers the role of gender in map-reading. 'Males,' it says, 'continue to demonstrate superior visual-spatial skills – the skills needed in order to read maps.'

F But not always. Sharon Carr-Brown, a radio researcher, resists becoming the reluctant navigator. 'I stopped that right at the beginning of our relationship. We actually fight over who drives. If it is a difficult journey I do the driving so that he can read the map, and he is very good at it,' she says.

G Another recent survey carried out by Relate/Candis, which focused on arguing, concluded that 'drawn-out bickering' was most likely to occur in the car. Add a map and an unfamiliar route and the bickering can lead to disaster.

Part 3

Read the following newspaper article and then answer questions **21–27** on page **27**.
Indicate the letter, **A, B, C** or **D** against the number of each question **21–27**.
Give only one answer to each question.

You could be one of those lucky people who seem to be naturally good at public speaking. It is unlikely that you were born with this ability. Great speakers are instinctive and inspired. They also prepare well, learn performance technique and draw heavily on experience to develop their skills.

What passes for a natural ease and rapport with an audience is often down to technique – the speaker using learned skills so well that we can't see the 'seams'.

Body language

You can learn to speak effectively in public by going on courses and reading manuals. But there is no substitute for getting out and doing it. If you dislike speaking in public, then take every opportunity to do so – even if you only start off by asking questions at the PTA meeting.

When you speak in public, almost all the aspects that make up your total image come under scrutiny. Your posture, body language, facial expression, use of voice and appearance all matter.

The situation is often stressful, because the speaker is being observed and judged by others. Small quirks, like speaking too quietly or wriggling, which are not particularly noticeable in everyday communication, become intrusive and exaggerated in front of an audience.

Stereotypes

It is hardly surprising, then, that some of us feel it is easier to pretend to be somebody else when we are speaking in public. We assume a 'public speaking image' that has nothing to do with our real selves.

We sense that speaking in public is connected to acting and so we portray

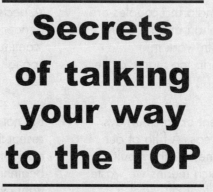

Secrets of talking your way to the TOP

stereotypical roles like 'the super-smooth sales person', 'the successful superwoman'. Unfortunately, if we don't really feel like these types, then we will look as though we are striving for effect.

By Philippa Davies
Managing Director of London-based communication specialists VOICEWORKS

For instance, you could decide that you want to play the life and soul of the party when you speak, although, in actuality, you are a rather quiet person who rarely uses humour. You read that humour works well in public speaking so you decide to tell a few jokes.

You look ill at ease when you do so and your timing leaves a lot to be desired. Your talk misfires badly. You will not have been true to yourself and your audience will have been reluctant to trust you. You need to find your own style.

The most skilled actors use their own feelings

and experiences to help them inhabit character. As a public speaker, you have more scope than most actors

– you have your own script, direction and interpretation to follow. You can even rearrange the set and choose the costume if you like.

The most successful speakers are obviously projecting an image but one that rings true. They project the best aspects of themselves – 'edited highlight'. The serious quiet person will project serenity and consideration for others. The outrageous extrovert will use humour and shock tactics. Speaking in public is a performance and one in which you present a heightened version of your personality.

To speak well, there needs to be a balance of impact between speaker, message and audience. If one of these elements overpowers the other two, say if the speaker is over-concerned to project personality, or the message is rammed home without due regard for the type of audience, or the speaker allows him or herself to be thrown by a noisy crowd – then the performance will suffer.

Image

Your image helps maintain this balance. If you get up to speak dressed like a Christmas tree, then your appearance will be overpowering. Delivering your message in an over-stressed and, therefore, over-significant tone of voice, will encourage your audience to switch off. When you start to speak, if your body language and facial expression remind the audience of a frightened rabbit, then you won't gain its confidence.

The biggest block to effective public speaking is attitude. If you think you can't and you never will be able to, you won't. Speaking in public is something anyone can learn to do. Be positive and accept setbacks as part of the learning process.

21 The author says that the best public speakers
    A are professional actors.
    B go on learning from the talks they give.
    C feel naturally at ease with people.
    D don't need to plan their talks in advance.

22 Her main advice to beginners is to
    A attend a course on public speaking.
    B ask good speakers for advice.
    C get as much practice as possible.
    D study other speakers' performances.

23 Some speakers pretend to be someone else because
    A they feel less self-conscious.
    B they don't want to be recognised.
    C they've been advised to.
    D they enjoy acting.

24 This approach is not recommended because
    A it will make the audience laugh.
    B it is likely to look false.
    C it can make the talk last too long.
    D the audience will complain.

25 The best speakers
    A use visual aids.
    B tell stories and jokes.
    C learn the scripts of their talks by heart.
    D present their most positive characteristics.

26 The author warns against
    A being too emphatic in what you say.
    B getting into arguments with the audience.
    C making the audience feel nervous.
    D wearing coloured clothing.

27 Overall, the author's message is that public speaking is
    A something few people can do.
    B the most frightening thing you can do.
    C a talent many people have naturally.
    D a skill that can be developed.

Part 4

Answer questions **28–47** by referring to the newspaper article about marine parks on page **29**.

> Remember to read the questions **before** you read the text in detail so you don't waste time on parts which aren't important.

> **▶ Questions 41 and 47**
>
> Look out for places where the information is expressed slightly differently in the text.

For questions **28–47** choose your answers from the list of places (**A–F**). Some choices may be required more than once.

Note: When more than one answer is required, these may be given **in any order**.

In which areas have the coral reefs been damaged by the following causes?

industry	28 ...F......		
dynamite fishing	29 ...P.....	30 ...F......	**A** Australia
Crown of Thorns starfish	31 ...A......	32 ...F......	
spear fishing	33 ...B......		
coral collecting or mining	34 ...D......	35 ...E......	**B** Cozumel, Mexico
	36		
pollution from resorts	37 ...D......		

Which areas offer the following attractions?

unique fish	38 ...C......		**C** Hawaii
good visibility	39 ...B......	40 ...F......	
good value diving	41 ...B......		**D** Maldives
snorkelling tours	42 ...A......	43 ...E......	
shark feeds	44 ...D......		
the fish with the longest name	45 ...C......		**E** Philippines

Which areas have the following problems?

There is overcrowding in some places	46 ...C......	**F** Thailand
It's expensive to get to the coral reefs	47 ...A......	

18/20

In search of the fish with the longest name

MARINE PARKS

Marine tourism – and conservation of coral reefs – is booming all over the tropics. NICK HANNA reports

A Australia

The Great Barrier Reef is the largest and most complex reef system on the planet. Its 2,900 individual reefs are divided up into a complex set of zones comprising the world's biggest marine park, home to more than 1,500 species of fish and 400 species of coral.

Since the reef is 30 to 45 miles offshore, most people visit on a day trip; these operate from resort islands as well as from Cairns, Port Douglas and Townsville. The cost of these trips can be prohibitive, and in this respect the Barrier Reef isn't as satisfying as somewhere, say, such as the Maldives, where you can just stumble out of your room and take a short swim to the reef at the edge of the lagoon.

A recent innovation in marine tourism here has been the introduction of guided snorkelling tours with marine biologists, which give you a 'hands-on' experience of the reef and an opportunity to touch corals and other marine life safely.

Like reefs all over the world, the Great Barrier is not without its share of ecological problems, the most notable of which, as we wrote two weeks ago, is the destruction caused by population outbreaks of Crown of Thorns starfish, which literally eat the reef.

B Cozumel, Mexico

Cozumel, a small island off Mexico's Yucatan peninsula, is another success story for marine parks. Although the island's reefs were popular with divers as long ago as the 1960s, the reef environment deteriorated badly in the 1970s through uncontrolled spear-fishing (which took care of the larger fish) and the harvesting of coral for the souvenir trade. However, thanks to the foresight of the Mexican government in declaring the reefs a marine refuge in 1980, fish populations are now thriving and divers are flocking there.

Cozumel is divided from the mainland by a deep-water channel which is swept by rich currents, ensuring not only flourishing marine flora and fauna, but also guaranteed good visibility (normally in excess of 100ft). The underwater terrain is unique in the Caribbean, with colossal coral buttresses riddled with caverns and tunnels.

Cozumel is to American divers what Egypt and the Red Sea are to their European counterparts: good-value, good-quality tropical diving: currently the best bargain in the Caribbean.

C Hawaii

The islands of the Hawaiian archipelago are the most isolated tropical islands in the world, which means that a high proportion of marine species are endemic. Many of these biologically unique fish are very beautiful indeed, and snorkelling or diving here is a distinctive experience.

On the main island of Oahu, Hanuama Bay is one of the most successful marine parks in Hawaii. Once a favourite fishing ground for Hawaiian royalty, the reefs were severely depleted until the area became a marine life conservation district in 1967. Since then, recovery has been remarkable, and there is now an abundance of beautiful tropical reef fish, including the fish with the longest name in the world, the Humuhumunukunukuapuaa (Hawaii's state emblem). The one drawback of Hanuama Bay is that the water is almost as crowded with people as it is with fish: go early in the morning.

D Maldives

Although there are no official marine parks or protected areas, the diving and snorkelling is generally superb. There are well-equipped dive centres on most tourist islands and snorkellers will find that in very few other countries is the magic of the underwater world as guaranteed as it is here. Large, tame fish abound on nearly every reef and in some lagoons you'll find yourself completely surrounded by what seems like a circular wall of fish, as if you were floating in a gigantic tropical aquarium.

Some reefs do have problems, most noticeably because of coral being mined for building, and pollution from resorts, but overall they appear to be in good shape.

Shark feeds are common in the Maldives, and many divers enjoy the opportunity to observe the power and grace of these magnificent creatures underwater.

E Philippines

There are more than 13,000 square miles of reefs in the Philippines but thanks to dynamite fishing, coral souvenirs and hurricanes, a considerable proportion are dead.

Although there are as yet no national marine parks, there are protected areas where you can find good diving and snorkelling. Some of the best reefs are around Palawan; at the diving resort of El Nido on the northwest corner of the island, they've made a concerted effort to protect their reefs, as well as setting up feeding stations, which are frequented by large groupers, jacks, needlefish and barracuda.

There is a cluster of dive resorts near Anilao, two hours south of Manila. Boats go out to Sombrero Island, a popular dive spot with surprisingly intact coral cover. This is one of the better dives I had in the Philippines: sadly, the exception rather than the rule.

F Thailand

The most extensive reefs in Thailand are in the Andaman Sea, on the west coast. This includes the area around Phuket, although many reefs in the immediate vicinity of Phuket have been smothered and killed by dredging for tin, which was the principal industry here before tourism.

Some of the best diving is in the Ko Similan National Park. Although there is some damage from dynamite fishing and Crown of Thorns starfish here, fish life is abundant enough to satisfy most people and visibility can reach 125ft-plus during the season. The best developed reefs are beyond the Similans in the Ko Surin National Park.

Reefs around Koh Samui and Koh Phangan on the east coast have been damaged by dynamite fishing and bottom trawling. Snorkelling trips operate from Koh Samui to the nearby Ang Thong National Park, but this suffers from similar problems and I found it disappointing.

Paper 2 – Writing

Part 1

1 After seeing an advert for a local restaurant, you and your friend Tony went there last Friday but it was an expensive and disappointing evening. You've described the experience in a letter to a friend.

Read the restaurant advertisement and bill below and the extract from the letter on page 31. Then, **using the information carefully,** write the letter as instructed on page 31.

The
Golden Fork
Restaurant

For an unforgettable evening of fine dining

Specialities:

- seafood
- vegetarian dishes
- steaks
- Indian curries
- game
- desserts

All our food is freshly prepared using only the finest ingredients.
Cosy atmosphere
Friendly staff
Reasonable prices

Telephone: 463271

The
Golden Fork
Restaurant

Table Number: 1
Date: 14/11

Steak	15.99
Vegetarian hot pot	12.99
Chocolate mousse	3.50
Cheesecake	2.50
House red	10.00
Coffee	2.50
Bread	1.00
	48.48
Service 20%	9.70
TOTAL	**£58.18**

Dear Pat,

You asked how Tony's birthday celebration went. Well, after discussing various options, we decided on a place called the Golden Fork, which advertises in the local paper, and also had a good review in our restaurant guide. All I can say is it's not a good idea to believe everything you read!

When we arrived, the place was empty – hardly a good sign! It was also absolutely freezing and we had to keep our coats on throughout. The menu looked quite promising, actually, but they were completely out of lobster which was our first choice. The waiter was pretty scruffy and off-hand and we got the distinct impression he was more interested in getting back to the kitchen where it was warmer! In the end, I had a steak which was as tough as old boots, with peas which were obviously tinned. Tony had some vegetarian dish which they'd obviously heated up in the microwave – even so it was lukewarm.

The bill was the last straw! It was <u>enormous</u> – they'd charged extra for bread (which we didn't eat), <u>and</u> included a service charge of 20%, would you believe it? In the end we just paid the bill and went, we were too miserable to make a fuss. Thinking about it later, though, and looking at what it says in their advert, we've decided to write and complain in the strongest terms. If they don't give us our money back, we're going to write to that restaurant guide and put them in the picture!

Now write a suitable **letter of complaint** to the Golden Fork Restaurant (approximately 250 words).

You should use your own words as far as possible.

Part 2

Choose **one** of the following writing tasks. Your answer should follow exactly the instructions given. Write approximately 250 words.

2 An English family are coming to live in your town for a year. This is part of a letter you receive from them.

> One thing we need to arrange is education for the children, John (5) and Alice (12). I'm afraid I know very little about the system in your country — could you give me some general information about the different levels, the school year, the school day, whether you have to pay for books, etc.? — and also suggest some schools I could contact to see if they've got places? If you could send it asap, I'd be really grateful.

Write a **report**.

3 An international students' magazine is running a series of articles on the things people collect, usual or unusual, and you have decided to submit a piece about your own hobby. Describe how your hobby started, what you find interesting or satisfying about it, and where you go to find additions to your collection. Mention any item which you are particularly pleased to have and/or that you would particularly like to have.

Write the **article**.

4 You have received this memo from the librarian at your school/college.

MEMO

From: B. Snary (Librarian)

To: All Staff and Students

Part of our budget each year is set aside for purchasing new additions to the library, which can be books, videos, or subscriptions to magazines/newspapers, and we invite you to suggest how this money should be spent.

Please send me your recommendations for one or more items, explaining clearly how these would be of benefit to the institution as a whole. Any other ideas as to how the library service could be improved would also be welcome.

Write a **proposal**.

5 You've just moved into a new flat, which will be very nice once it's re-decorated. You can't afford to employ a professional decorator so you'd like to organise a 'painting party' where your friends will help you. Write a letter which you can copy to a number of friends telling them about the flat and your idea for a party. Try to persuade them that it would be fun to come along and lend a hand.

Write the **letter**.

Paper 3 – English in Use

Part 1

For questions **1–15**, read the article below and then decide which word on page **35** best fits each space. Circle the letter you choose for each question. The exercise begins with an example (**0**).

Example:

Save money on the book that aims to save animals

Do you want to (**0**) ... part in the battle to save the world's wildlife? *Animal Watch* is a book which will (**1**) ... you in the fight for survival that (**2**) ... many of our endangered animals and show how they struggle on the (**3**) ... of extinction. As you enjoy the book's 250 pages and over 150 colour photographs, you will have the (**4**) ... of knowing that part of your purchase money is being used to (**5**) ... animals (**6**) ... . From the comfort of your armchair, you will be able to observe the world's animals close-up and explore their habitats. You will also discover the terrible results of human (**7**) ... for land, flesh and skins.

Animal Watch is packed with fascinating facts. Did you know that polar bears cover their black noses (**8**) ... their (**9**) ... so they can hunt their prey in the snow without being seen, for example? Or that (**10**) ... each orang-utan which is captured, one has to die?

This superb (**11**) ... has so (**12**) ... Britain's leading wildlife charity that it has been chosen as Book of the Year, a (**13**) ... awarded to books which are considered to have made a major contribution to wildlife conservation. You will find *Animal Watch* at a special low (**14**) ... price at all good bookshops, but hurry while (**15**) ... last.

0	A play	B be	C take	D have
1	A combine	B involve	C bring	D lead
2	A meets	B opposes	C forces	D faces
3	A edge	B start	C limit	D end
4	A satisfaction	B enjoyment	C virtue	D value
5	A enable	B help	C allow	D assist
6	A preserve	B conserve	C revive	D survive
7	A greed	B interest	C care	D concern
8	A with	B by	C for	D from
9	A feet	B claws	C paws	D toes
10	A with	B by	C for	D from
11	A publicity	B periodical	C publication	D reference
12	A imposed	B impressed	C persuaded	D admired
13	A symbol	B title	C trademark	D nickname
14	A beginning	B preparatory	C original	D introductory
15	A stores	B stocks	C goods	D funds

13/15

Part 2

For questions **16–30**, complete the following article by writing each missing word in the space provided. **Use only one word for each space.** The exercise begins with an example (**0**).

Example: | 0 | by | | 0 |

Olympic Gold

In April 1896, an Irishman (**0**) .... the name of John Pius Boland was in Athens visiting the famous German archaeologist, Schliemann, (**16**) .... it came to his ears that there was a sporting event (**17**) .... place in the city. Being a keen tennis player, he decided to investigate further and discovered (**18**) .... his surprise that the event in question was none other (**19**) .... the first ever Modern Olympic Games and that (**20**) .... a variety of events it included a tennis tournament. (**21**) .... only of modest standard, he borrowed a pair of white flannel trousers and a racquet, entered and won the gold medal. Encouraged by his success, he teamed up in the Men's Doubles (**22**) .... a German, Fritz Krauern, and won that too – thereby earning himself a place in the record books (**23**) .... the first man to share an Olympic gold medal with (**24**) .... of another nationality.

'The important thing in the Olympic Games is not winning (**25**) .... taking part,' declared the founder of the Modern Olympics, the Baron de Coubertin. Doubtless (**26**) .... who fought well and won in those first Games felt every bit (**27**) .... satisfied with their achievements as any of today's medal-hungry competitors when the time came to line (**28**) .... in front of a table and step forward to receive their rewards. (The victory podium incidentally, along (**29**) .... flags and national anthems, was not introduced (**30**) .... the Los Angeles Games of 1932.)

When

From *High Life*

Part 3

In **most** lines of the following text there is **one** unnecessary word. It is either grammatically incorrect or does not fit in with the sense of the text. For each numbered line **31–46**, write the **unnecessary** word in the spaces next to the question number below. Some lines are correct. Indicate these lines with a tick (✔). The exercise begins with two examples (**0**).

Examples:

0	the		0
0	✔		0

THE BIG SLEEP

0	Since the time immemorial we have put our trust in a good night's
0	sleep to help us look and feel better. And with good reason: sleep
31	restores the body, builds out muscle, strengthens bones and the
32	immune system and helps with skin cells to regenerate. But just
33	how much sleep do we really need is a matter of debate. Back in
34	the 9th century King Alfred the Great was the first to decide that a
35	third of the day – eight hours – should be spent in asleep. Though
36	we still use Alfred's idea as a yardstick, but we all find the sleep
37	patterns which suit us best. While it's true that too much or too
38	little of sleep can cause headaches, drowsiness, lack of energy
39	and irritability, it's the *quality* of sleep or rather than the quantity,
40	which are matters. Since man's earliest days, all sorts of medicines
41	and drugs have been tried to achieve deep, untroubled sleep.
42	However, to get away from artificial methods, the exercising during
43	the day and avoiding such indigestible food, caffeine-filled drinks
44	and alcohol just before bedtime can help you to sleep better. And
45	the right kind environment is very important. You need to be in
46	darkness, warm – but not too warm – and be comfortable.

31	35	39	43 ....
32	36	40	44 ....
33	37	41	45 ....
34	38	42	46 ....

Part 4

For questions **47–61** read the two texts below. Use the words in the boxes to the right of the texts, listed **47–61**, to form a word that fits in the same numbered space in the text. The exercise begins with an example **(0)**.

Example: | 0 | *competitive* | | 0 |

GOLF

6/14

Golf is a popular **(0)** ... game, played by people of a wide range of age and **(47)** ... . **(48)** ... many other activities, golf retains its players throughout their lifetime – players in their eighties claim the game helps keep them fit and **(49)** ... alert. Golf strengthens the back and shoulders and helps to maintain spine **(50)** ... . However, the game does require a **(51)** ... good level of fitness to reduce the risk of injuring yourself – stretching exercises for the **(52)** ... body and legs, strengthening exercises for the shoulders, and weight training to strengthen the forearm and wrist are important. Golfers also need to do aerobic exercise such as jogging or cycling to give them sufficient **(53)** ... .

(0)	COMPETE
(47)	ABLE
(48)	LIKE
(49)	MENTAL
(50)	ROTATE
(51)	REASON
(52)	UP
(53)	ENDURE

JOGGING

Slow, relaxed, **(54)** ... running is an excellent exercise for cardiovascular fitness and weight control. It requires no special skill, little expenditure, and can be done almost anywhere. But **(55)** ... jogging, especially on hard surfaces, can result in **(56)** ... to the joints and muscles. Regular jogging also tends to **(57)** ... and **(58)** ... muscles because movements take place through a restricted range and are repeated many times. This makes it important to perform stretching exercises to maintain the **(59)** ... of the muscles most at risk. To get the greatest benefit and **(60)** ... the risks, it is best to increase your **(61)** ... distance slowly, by no more than 10–20 per cent every two weeks.

(54)	CONTINUE
(55)	EXCEED
(56)	INJURE
(57)	SHORT
(58)	TIGHT
(59)	FLEXIBLE
(60)	MINIMUM
(61)	WEEK

47	52	57 ....
48	53	58 ....
49	54	59 ....
50	55	60 ....
51	56	61 ....

Part 5

For questions **62–74**, read the following details of booking conditions from a travel brochure and use the information to complete the numbered gaps in the informal note to a friend. **Use no more than two words** for each gap. The words which you need **do not occur** in the booking conditions. The exercise begins with an example (**0**).

Example: | **0** | *arrange* | | **0** |

BOOKING CONDITIONS

1. Reservations
Reservations should be made through your travel agent, at least 14 days in advance. Late bookings, up to three days in advance, can be accepted but are subject to availability of accommodation and flights. We suggest that late bookings be accompanied by full payment to expedite preparation of travel documents.

2. Visas
Tour participants must ensure that they comply with all visa and health requirements of countries they intend to visit. If in doubt, tour participants are advised to consult their travel agent.

3. Amendments
Tour itineraries may be extended in duration and additional sightseeing tours may be included. Please ask your travel agent for extra night rates and Optional Tour prices. All modifications and extensions must be made at the time of booking. Changes made after travel documents have been issued are subject to an amendment fee of US $50. No changes can be made after departure.

INFORMAL NOTE

Jane – Re: the holiday

I've been looking through the brochure again and I think we'd better act fast. We have to (**0**) .... things through a travel agent, so I'll call in to 'Worldwide Tours' tomorrow. As it's less than a (**62**) .... before the departure date, it all (**63**) .... whether they can (**64**) .... us hotels and flights for the dates we want. Apparently, at this late stage it's (**65**) .... to pay the whole (**66**) .... rather than just the deposit, so they can get the tickets and things (**67**) .... as quickly as possible.

The brochure says it's (**68**) .... us to make sure we have all the (**69**) .... visas and injections. That's something I'll (**70**) .... with the travel agent. There's a note in the small print to say you can make the trip a bit (**71**) .... if you want, and there are some extra sightseeing tours you can (**72**) .... do. We'd have to decide now, though, because they (**73**) .... an extra fee to change the tickets later and you can't make any changes once the trip (**74**) ....

Lyn

Part 6

For questions **75–80**, read through the following text and then choose from the list **A–J** the best phrase given below it to fill each of the spaces. Write one letter (**A–J**) in each space provided. **Some of the suggested answers do not fit at all.** The exercise begins with an example (**0**).

Example: | 0 | J | | 0 |

Migraine Headaches

Nearly everyone has had a headache at some time or another – and if it is only an occasional thing you won't need to seek help from your doctor. The most common type of headache, which affects 80 per cent of people at some stage of their lives, is the tension headache. (**0**) ...

(**75**) ... It is now known that during an attack measurable changes take place in chemicals in the body which are not seen in other types of headache. (**76**) ... In between attacks you feel completely well. The headaches usually last up to three days and often affect only one side of the head. You feel sick and you can't stand bright lights. And when the attack is over many people feel totally washed out.

Although there are five identifiable stages of a migraine attack, not everyone experiences all of them, and no two people will have attacks of the same duration, frequency and severity. (**77**) ...
They can become more frequent and more severe for no apparent reason, or stop for several months or even years.

Migraine seems to be caused by an inherited susceptibility, combined with a response to certain internal and external factors. (**78**) ... The triggers of a migraine attack are many and varied, but most of them, in excess, can harm the body. For example, lack of food: the body needs fuel and cannot go too long without it. (**79**) ...

Although there is no absolute cure for migraine, it can be controlled. Discovering your own triggers and dealing with them can help you have fewer attacks, and put you in control. (**80**) ...

From *The Sunday Express Magazine*

A Even within each person, attacks change with time.
B The same applies to lack of sleep.
C An attack is your body's way of letting you know that you are pushing things a little too far.
D Or the pain can be quite vague and may be present most of the day with little change.
E Migraine, however, is something different.
F Remember, bad habits can be overcome.
G Others have times when they get as many as two attacks a week.
H Unlike tension headaches, migraine attacks do not occur daily.
I It is very rare to have an attack over the age of 40.

J Hunger, sleeping in or being overtired are other factors which can cause headaches.

Paper 4 – Listening

Part 1

You will hear some information about home security. For questions **1–9**, fill in the missing information.

You will hear the recording twice.

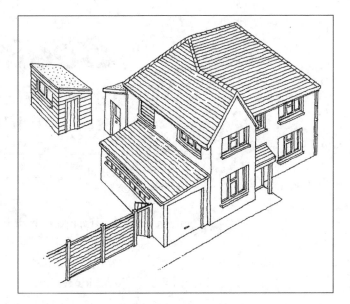

Area	Problem	Solution
Doors	Inadequate locks can be	Fit strong locks
	1	
Windows	Downstairs windows provide the burglar with	Fit strong locks
	2	
	Upstairs windows can be reached with	Fit strong locks
	3	
	Louvre windows have glass panels which	Fit lock or replace with
	4	5
Garage or garden shed	Can provide useful	Fit a strong padlock or
	6	7
Porch	If unlit, callers cannot be	Install a special
	8	9

Part 2

You will hear about a competition for young writers. As you listen, complete the information for questions **10–17**.

Listen very carefully as you will hear the recording ONCE only.

Bookworm
Young Writers' Competition
Rules

- Open to children aged [_____ **10**] on the closing date.

- An entry can be poetry, prose or drama, but it must be
  [_____ **11**] piece of writing.

- Entries should be no longer than [_____ **12**] words.

- Each entry must accompanied by a [_____ **13**]
  from a parent or teacher certifying that the work was written unaided.

- All sheets must be numbered and [_____ **14**]

- Entries must be sent to the following address:

  Young Writers' Competition

  [_____ **15**]

  TAUNTON

  Somerset TA1 5QT

- No entries will [_____ **16**]

- The **closing date** is [_____ **17**]

Part 3

You will hear an interview with Robert Miles who works as a Flight Service Director for an airline. For questions **18–29** complete each of the statements.

You will hear the recording twice.

What Robert enjoys about his job is travelling and

_____ **18** different people.

What he doesn't enjoy about his job are the _____ **19**

In his previous career, he worked in the _____ **20**

He originally intended to stay with the airline for

_____ **21**

He gets between _____ **22** days off during
a working period.

By working in Cabin Crew Management, he finds out what goes on

_____ **23** in other departments.

His most famous passenger has been _____ **24**

He feels the best way to help nervous passengers is to

_____ **25** them.

He also takes them on to _____ **26** so they can see
what goes on.

The passengers who make his life difficult are those who make

_____ **27**

When he started in his job, it was possible to offer passengers a more

_____ **28** .

The other change is that nowadays he has to

_____ **29** sectors.

Part 4

You will hear five short extracts in which various people are talking about bargains they have bought.

TASK ONE

For questions **30–34**, match the extracts as you hear them with the things the speakers bought, listed **A–H**.

A an oil painting

B a wardrobe

C a motorcycle

D a typewriter

E an exercise bike

F a rug

G a table

H a car

	30
	31
	32
	33
	34

TASK TWO

For questions **35–39**, match the extracts as you hear them with the reasons the original owners sold things cheaply, listed **A–H**.

A They needed to sell it quickly.

B They couldn't afford to keep it.

C They didn't have enough room for it.

D They didn't like it.

E They knew it was faulty.

F They didn't realise it was valuable.

G They didn't know how to use it.

H They had never used it.

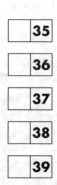

	35
	36
	37
	38
	39

**Remember that you must complete both tasks as you listen.
You will hear the recording twice.**

Paper 5 – Speaking

Work with another student.

Part 1 (3 minutes) Introductions and General Social Conversation

Imagine you had never met your partner.

* Introduce yourselves to each other.

* Tell your partner a little bit about yourself. Listen to what your partner says and ask one or two questions.

* Find out why your partner is learning English. Explain your own reasons.

* Tell your partner about a special interest or hobby of yours. Find out what interests your partner has.

Part 2 (3 or 4 minutes)

In this part of the test you will each have the opportunity to talk for a minute.

Task 1

Then and Now (Describe and contrast)

You should both look at the same pair of pictures. They both show the same family members but they were taken several years apart.

Turn to the pictures on page 145.

Candidate A: Talk about both the pictures to your partner and comment on the main changes that have taken place over the years. You have about one minute for this.

Candidate B: Listen carefully to your partner's descriptions and then say which age you would prefer to be, and why.

Task 2

Fashions from the Past (Describe and identify)

You will each have a set of pictures showing fashions from the past. Don't look at each other's pictures.

Candidate B: Turn to the pictures on page 146. Choose two pictures and describe them so that your partner can identify them. You have about one minute for this.

Candidate A: Turn to the pictures on page 145. Listen carefully to your partner's description and decide which two pictures are being described. If you still need help at the end, you can ask your partner one or two questions. Are you interested in fashion? Why/why not?

Part 3 (3 or 4 minutes)

Evolution (Interpret and discuss)

In this part of the test you have to discuss a topic with your partner.

Look at the cartoon below. Talk about the four parts and decide what point the cartoonist is making. Do you agree with the cartoonist's point of view? Why/why not?

You have three or four minutes for this.

Part 4 (3 or 4 minutes)

In this part of the test you and your partner have to report on the outcome of your discussion in Part 3, saying whether you agreed or not. You then take part in a more general discussion with your partner and the examiner.

Practise your reporting and discussion skills by working with another pair. Take it in turns to summarise and explain the conclusions you reached, and then discuss the following questions:

- Do people watch too much television today?

- What are the most worthwhile kinds of programme?

- Does television have a harmful effect on children? Why/why not?

- Are there any better ways of relaxing?

▶ Answer Key

Practice Test 1

Paper 1

Part 1

1 E	4 A	8/9 C/F	12 G
2 H	5 G	10 H	13/14 A/C
3 B	6/7 B/D	11 B	

Part 2

15 E	17 G	19 A
16 B	18 F	20 C

Part 3

21 B	23 A	25 D	27 D
22 C	24 B	26 A	

Part 4

28 F	29/30 E/F	31/32 A/F	33 B
34/35/36 B/D/E	37 D	38 C	39/40 B/F
41 B	42/43 A/F	44 D	45 C
46 C	47 A		

Paper 2

See notes on marking and assessment criteria on page 10.

Paper 3

Part 1

0 C (example)

1 B	5 B	9 C	13 B
2 D	6 D	10 C	14 D
3 A	7 A	11 C	15 B
4 A	8 A	12 B	

Part 2

0 by (example)   16 when   17 taking
18 to   19 than   20 among(st)
21 (Al)though   22 with   23 as
24 someone   25 but   26 those/someone/anyone
27 as   28 up   29 with   30 until

Part 3

0 the (example)
0 ✓ (example)

31 out	35 in	39 or	43 such
32 with	36 but	40 are	44 ✓
33 do	37 ✓	41 ✓	45 kind
34 ✓	38 of	42 the	46 be

Part 4

47 ability	52 upper	57 shorten
48 Unlike	53 endurance	58 tighten
49 mentally	54 continuous	59 flexibility
50 rotation	55 excessive	60 minimise
51 reasonably	56 injuries	61 weekly

Part 5

0 arrange (example)   62 fortnight
63 depends (on)   64 find/get
65 advisable/sensible/best   66 amount
67 ready/to us   68 up to   69 necessary
70 check (on)   71 longer   72 choose to
73 charge   74 has begun/started

Part 6

0 J (example)

75 E	77 A	79 B
76 H	78 C	80 F

Paper 4

Part 1

1 easily opened   2 (easy) access   3 a ladder
4 slide out   5 ordinary windows
6 equipment for burglars   7 remove tools
8 identified   9 security light

Part 2

10 16 or under   11 an original   12 3,500
13 signed statement   14 pinned together
15 PO Box 2000   16 be returned
17 September 12th

Part 3

18 looking after   19 long hours
20 public service   21 2/two years
22 18/eighteen and 28/twenty-eight
23 behind the scenes   24 the Queen
25 reassure   26 the flight deck
27 unreasonable demands
28 personalised/personal service   29 fly longer

Part 4

30 F	33 G	36 H	39 C
31 E	34 D	37 A	
32 H	35 D	38 F	

Practice Test 2

Paper 1 – Reading

Part 1

Answer questions **1–16** by referring to the newspaper article about people who work for VSO (Voluntary Service Overseas) on page **49**.

For questions **1–16**, answer by choosing from the list (**A–F**) on the right below. Some of the choices may be required more than once.

Note: When more than one answer is required, these may be given **in any order**.

Which volunteer(s)

wasn't confident of their ability to do the work required?	1 ....C....		**A** Elizabeth Smith
later took responsibility for raising money to help VSO?	2 ....E....		
has learnt how some of their former students are getting on?	3 ...A....	4 ...D...	
was afraid of some local wildlife?	5 ...B....		**B** Adriane Hughes
suffered from health problems?	6 ....E–A....		
has revisited the place where they were originally posted?	7 ...D....	8 ...B E...	**C** Larry O'Donnell
mentions severe weather conditions in the area where they worked?	9 ...C....		
had few skills and little experience when they were posted overseas?	10 ...D....		**D** Chris Tipple
was happy to work without sophisticated equipment?	11 ...A....		
carried out construction work of various kinds?	12 ...A C....		**E** Dick Bird
is concerned about arrangements for accommodation?	13 ...F....		
recalls how friendly the local people were?	14 ...B....		**F** Anne Landolt
warns that working for VSO can have its problems?	15 ...E....		
mentions a valuable lesson learnt by a volunteer?	16 ...A....		

Question 1

Look for an alternative way of saying this.

Question 6

Look for the mention of a particular disease. The information is in the first reference to this person.

Question 9

Think of another expression which refers to the weather conditions in a particular area.

13/16

▼
Notice that most volunteers are mentioned more than once. You may find it helpful to go through the text highlighting the names, so that you don't miss any references.

The quiet crusaders

It's a tough job and fewer people want to do it. But VSO still attracts a special kind of person, says **Michael Booth.**

I LIKE to think that in my 26 years on this earth I have seen a few things. But recently I've been talking to a handful of the 22,000 Voluntary Service Overseas (VSO) volunteers past and present who have been flung far by this extraordinary organisation, and it has proved to be something of a disheartening experience.

Take **Elizabeth Smith**, who, as a tutor of nurses in northern Zambia, found herself tending the wounds of a man mauled by a hippo, and twice contracted malaria. Or **Adriane Hughes**, who spent two years in Malawi teaching book-keeping to beekeepers. Or **Larry O'Donnell**, who went from making kitchen units to building pre-fabricated warehouses to house refugee camps on the Sudanese border.

Chris Tipple, now Director of Education for Northumberland, was among the first VSO recruits in 1958, spending seven months as a teacher in Ghana. The earliest recruits like him left with no training and little idea of what awaited. But youth and innocence were soon found to be inadequate. "Many countries were declaring independence at the time and launching into huge schemes of education, health care and infrastructure," says **Dick Bird**, VSO's director of fund-raising, and himself a former recruit. "The first volunteers came back saying it had been a great experience, but really there was a serious job to be done in developing countries, and people with more skills and experience were needed." These days VSO only accepts qualified and skilled recruits, aged 20 to 70.

Recruits are getting harder to find. Fewer applications are received each year, and only 50 per cent of requests from foreign countries are met.

Two who recommend the experience are **Elizabeth Smith** and **Larry O'Donnell**. "Working for 10 years in a cardiology department made me feel I had come to rely on machines too much. I wanted to do some work without the technology propping me up," says Elizabeth, 33. "Most of my students have written to me since saying I inspired them to do further training, which was terrifically rewarding. You can learn practical things, too.

A pharmacist I know saw sugar paste being used as dressings for burns in Africa and now uses it in a hospital in the UK."

Larry, 35, left behind his job and family for his posting. "It was a wrench, but it was exciting and challenging. I did have doubts about my professional abilities, and the climate in the Sudan was harsh, but it changed the course of my life. Completing a contract for Save The Children, building school climbing frames, was probably the most rewarding thing I did."

Anne Landolt, 28, from Kent, has it all ahead of her. She is about to leave for Ghana for a two-year posting as a water and sanitation engineer.

"I'm worried about how I am going to get on with the people out there," she admits, "and I've got nowhere to live yet. They've told me I might have to sleep on a classroom floor." Like all volunteers, Anne will have her travel expenses covered by VSO and receive a grant of £2,300 over the two years.

She can also take comfort from **Adriane Hughes**, who returned in December from one of the more bizarre postings. Hughes, 50, owned a flourishing training consultancy business before giving it all up for a posting to Malawi.

"I wanted to do something more worthwhile than just be a tourist," she explains. "My job was to visit 108 beekeeping clubs in the Niyika National Park. They'd been set up to allow people to earn a living from the park, where there had been a lot of poaching. I was there to show them how to run the clubs as a business."

Adriane admits that the bees "frightened the hell out of me". But there were greater concerns. "I was sent to live in a township with 10,000 Malawians, with machetes, which was very daunting. But actually I felt safe all the time and was made very welcome."

Chris Tipple recently returned to Africa to find out what effect, if any, his stint abroad had on those they left behind. "I addressed the assembly at my old school, which was an emotional experience," says Chris. "I also met eight of my old students – they were almost the same age as me, of course. One man is now owner of a chemical company and another woman has just retired as chief auditor to the Ghanaian Bank."

And when **Dick Bird** went back to the area where he had worked, he met the Malawian who was now doing his job, "So I felt that, 35 years on, there had been progress. The work was being done by a local. I would never say to anyone that a VSO posting will all go smoothly. But I *would* say don't hesitate. Do it."

Part 2

For questions **17–22**, you must choose which of the paragraphs **A–G** on page **51** fit into the numbered gaps in the following newspaper article. There is one extra paragraph which does not fit in any of the gaps.

BACK-CHAT

If your heart skips a beat when you realise you are about to talk to an answering machine you most definitely aren't alone.

17

Top psychologist Dr David Lewis has examined what lies behind the problem that appears to be peculiar to us Britons, and now offers some solutions. Logic points to our typically reserved nature as the main reason for our lack of confidence when faced with answering machines. Our American cousins certainly have no trouble talking to machines (14 per cent of Americans have answering machines against two or three per cent in the UK).

18

So, are past problems in dealing with answering machines putting off these potential owners – despite the fact that they realise the enormous benefits? Dr Lewis has looked at the phenomenon in some depth. He has identified six main fears which make talking to answering machines difficult, and has come up with some helpful tips on how to conquer each.

• Technophobia is experienced by people who have an inherent fear of machines of all types. Technophobes can easily be identified by conversations which develop in this way: "Hello, oh no, don't tell me I'm talking to a machine ... oh ... oh ... call me back."

19

• Some people have problems with answering machines because they need constant feedback during a conversation even if only with grunts of understanding and/or approval.

20

• Other people encounter difficulties with machines because they need time to warm up to a conversation. This applies to tough calls as well as casual chats. The machine inhibits them because they feel unable to ramble on.

21

• The element of time pressure can cause problems for some. Worrying that the machine won't allow enough time for you to say all you need can cause anxiousness and, in turn, key points of the message are forgotten. In this instance Dr Lewis suggests imagining the person you want to talk to is at the other end of the phone. He also recommends writing down what you intend to say until you become used to answering machines.

• The realisation that mistakes you make will be recorded on tape can make people nervous. This is most likely to occur in those with little confidence. Dr Lewis recommends assessing your performance and giving yourself positive feedback after leaving a message.

22

• Concern over errors can be a very real fear and is especially likely in people who always need to be assured that facts and figures are fully understood. With a machine, they worry about ambiguities distorting the message. In this case Dr Lewis recommends keeping the message as short as possible, and spelling any tricky words.

▶ **Question 20**

The clue here is in the section before: *they need constant feedback ...*

▶ **Question 18**

There are two clues to help you. One is in the section before: *two or three per cent* – is this a lot of people? The other is in the following section: *these potential owners* – **which** potential owners?

From *This is Bristol and Bath*

A Yet even though there's still only a small number of actual owners, a third of those questioned admitted they would find it useful to have an answering machine at home.

B Denied this kind of reassuring response, they tend to lose the thread of their conversations. To overcome this problem, Dr Lewis suggests practising by speaking into a tape recorder – especially if you are someone who comes across answering machines at work.

C Analyse how you did and, where there was a problem, try to work out a better way of responding for next time. If you own a machine yourself, listen to how respondents on your machine leave their messages and copy the best styles.

D Again, by planning calls, trouble can be avoided. The message should be kept short and simple and you should always include an action which you want taken such as "call me back" or "await a further call from me".

E There are now many products on the market, and each new product incorporates more advanced technology. Several of the newest machines, for instance, include a remote turn-on facility that allows you to switch them on with a simple call from anywhere in the world.

F Recent research conducted for British Telecom reveals that in the so-called age of technology, a staggering 45 per cent of people felt ill at ease when talking to answering machines. And a further 30 per cent of those questioned actually admitted rehearsing what they wanted to say before making a call.

G To help these sufferers Dr Lewis recommends planning messages carefully whenever you need to make a call. If you are caught unawares ring off, write down the key points – and then redial. You must be sure to give your name, phone number, the date and the time as well as a brief message.

Part 3

Read the following newspaper article and then answer questions **23–28** on page **53**.
Indicate the letter **A**, **B**, **C** or **D** against the number of each question **23–28**.
Give only one answer to each question.

Remember to look through the questions to see which parts of the text you need to read more carefully. Don't waste time on unimportant parts.

▶ **Paragraph 8**

It isn't necessary to understand the expression *to tread on someone's toes* in order to answer question 26, but it's a useful idiom and you may like to look it up afterwards.

How to help parents cope with homework

THE parents from hell may be the ones who make all the headlines, but research for a BBC series starting tonight showed that government ministers may be pushing on an open door in their quest for more parental involvement, in primary schools at least. Four out of five parents accepted that they should be more involved in their children's learning, even though two thirds claimed to be giving at least two hours a week.

More surprising, perhaps, was teachers' apparent enthusiasm for parental involvement. Not long ago, schools seemed to associate parents with intrusion into their territory: spying in the classroom and misdirecting children at home, especially where early reading skills were concerned.

Now the government's spotlight on performance has left teachers with little choice but to embrace all the help they can get. Nine out of ten told the BBC that parents should spend more time helping their children to learn at home, and three quarters thought that more than an hour a week was needed.

Teachers said they would like parents to spend more time reading, practising tables and taking their children on educational visits. One in five thought that simply having conversations with their children would be beneficial.

A new study of primary school literacy by Professor Ted Wragg and three colleagues at Exeter University, to be published next week, confirms teachers' acceptance of parental help with reading, although it acknowledges that "sceptics" remain. Some saw a partnership in literacy as the key to the good home/school relationship that most experts see as essential to smooth progress.

But the authors add: "Some teachers were concerned that parental effort would be inhibited by insufficient knowledge and experience to tackle the complicated task of teaching a child to read, particularly in terms of being up to date, or sharing beliefs with teachers." One interviewee cautioned that many parents did not realise that "things had moved on" since their time at school.

Yet there is still uncertainty about how to use time most productively. The parents among the BBC's 2,800 interviewees played wordgames with their children, read to them, watched educational programmes, helped with counting and played computer games. Any assistance with homework came on top.

Of those who said they would like to do more, a shortage of time was the most common explanation for not doing so, but one in ten admitted that they did not know how to help. Some felt that they would be treading on the teacher's toes to do more than the minimum, others were afraid of being considered pushy.

The *DynaMo* series, which is part of the BBC's Learning Zone, the overnight service designed for videotaping, should help to overcome such anxieties. The eight programmes, backed up by activity

▶ **Paragraph 12**

You may not know the expression *to beg a question* but you should be able to guess the meaning from the context: to raise a question about something which has not been dealt with in a satisfactory manner.

books and two websites, concentrate on literacy and numeracy, the government's overriding priorities for primary education.

Complete with obligatory cartoon characters to stimulate children's interest, the programmes have been developed in line with the government's strategies. As well as a free parents' guide, there are separate books for the under-sevens and those up to nine.

Since the children taking part in the research voted the cartoon character

Homer Simpson their ideal teacher, the cartoon presenters may have been a good idea. But the presence of their own parents (as well as their teachers) in the top five shows that most children welcome some help at home.

One question begged by the BBC's laudable initiative, however, is what happens beyond the age of nine? Parents are even more anxious about the possibility of showing themselves up when the work gets harder. The scope for a follow-up is obvious.

From The Times

▶ **Questions 23, 24 & 26**

When questions include words like *most* or *main*, make sure your answer is true in the majority of cases, not just for one or two.

23   According to research, how do most parents react to the government's attempt to involve them in their children's education?
   A   They believe they already help their children enough.
   B   They will need persuasion to help their children more.
   C   They agree that the initiative is right in principle.
   D   They resent any government interference in their lives.

24   The same research suggested that most teachers
   A   think that parents may give their children the wrong kind of help.
   B   are afraid that parents will interfere in their work at school.
   C   are more prepared to accept parental help than in the past.
   D   believe that parents should talk to their children more.

25   One concern expressed by a teacher in the Exeter University study was that parents
   A   might be unaware of developments in primary education.
   B   might be unable to read and write themselves.
   C   would be unwilling to keep up the hard work for long enough.
   D   would be unlikely to co-operate with teachers.

26   What was the main reason parents gave for not helping their children more?
   A   They thought it was the teacher's job, not theirs.
   B   They weren't sure of the best way to help.
   C   They didn't want their children to work too hard.
   D   They had too many other things to do.

27   The new television series has been designed to
   A   give parents training in modern teaching techniques.
   B   help children with reading, writing and arithmetic.
   C   provide information about government educational policies.
   D   entertain children with popular cartoon characters.

28   What seems to be the writer's opinion of the series?
   A   It's a good idea which should also be developed for older children.
   B   Although it's a good idea, it's designed for the wrong age group.
   C   It's likely to make parents more worried about helping their children.
   D   It's not challenging enough to keep children interested.

Part 4

Answer questions **29–48** by referring to the newspaper article about natural remedies on page **55**.

For questions **29–48** choose your answers from the list of natural remedies (**A–G**). Some choices may be required more than once.

Note: When more than one answer is required, these may be given **in any order**.

Which natural remedy or remedies

seems to help people recover from colds more quickly?	**29** .... E	**30** .... F	**A** St John's Wort
is believed by some doctors to help allergy sufferers?	**31** .... B	**32**	
has been tested in the USA?	**33** .... F	**34** .... G	**B** Pycnogenol
shouldn't be taken without medical supervision?	**35** .... A		
can be found in cabbages and cauliflowers?	**36** .... D C a		**C** Grape-Seed Extracts
is completely safe to take if you aren't allergic to it?	**37** .... D		
reduces the risk of heart disease?	**38** .... G		**D** Garlic
is recommended for treating depression?	**39** .... A		
seems to boost the immune system?	**40** .... D	**41** .... E	**E** Echinacea
may be helpful for cigarette smokers?	**42** .... B		
has been used for many hundreds of years?	**43** .... D	**44** .... A	**F** Zinc
can be found in prawns, lobsters and also beef?	**45** .... G F		
is more popular now than it was in the past?	**46** .... E		**G** Omega-3 Fatty Acids
may have harmful side-effects if taken in large doses?	**47** .... E	**48** .... A	

▶ **Questions 35 and 45**

In these questions you need to think of a general term which includes the specific examples given.

▶ **Question 46**

Remember that the information in the text may be expressed slightly differently.

Feel Better Naturally

By Anita Bartholomew

To keep yourself fighting fit delve into nature's medicine chest

Britons are downing a record number of nutritional supplements, spending more than £1 billion a year. Researchers maintain that you should get most of your nutrients from a well-balanced diet. But they also say that there may be real benefits to some natural remedies. Here are some of the most promising:

A St John's Wort

What it is: The wild variety of this herb, which is available in most health-food shops, has been used for centuries to calm the mind and heal the body.

What it does: St John's Wort is an antidepressant, effective for about two-thirds of those who try it. It has been prescribed by doctors in Germany for many years. Last year the British Medical Journal published an analysis of 23 clinical trials of the herb. It found that St John's Wort was effective for patients with mild to moderate depression. In addition, fewer patients using the herbal remedy reported minor side-effects than those taking prescription medicine.

Who should take it? If you have been feeling 'down' for a while, you might consider St John's Wort. Though the herb is sold without a prescription, experts agree that it should be taken under a doctor's supervision – especially if you have been taking an antidepressant or any other prescription drug. High doses of the drug may also cause sun sensitivity.

B Pycnogenol and C Grape-Seed Extracts

What they are: While these two herbal products come from different plants – Pycnogenol [pik-NAH-jeh-nal] is a registered brand name made from French Maritime pine bark; the other comes from grapes – each is a rich source of flavonoids, antioxidants protecting against free radicals that damage cells and tissue.

What they do: Flavonoids, which occur naturally in fruit and vegetables, work to keep cells healthy. Some doctors say that Pycnogenol and grape-seed extracts seem to ease the symptoms of inflammatory diseases and relieve allergies. And in a yet-to-be published study of the effects of Pycnogenol on young smokers, it reduced blood platelet clumping, a dangerous artery-clogging effect of smoking.

Who should take them? If you don't always eat the recommended five servings a day of fruit and vegetables, you might consider taking one of these extracts.

D Garlic

What it is: A member of the onion family, it has been used as a medicinal herb since the time of the ancient Egyptians.

What it does: European studies show that in cultures where people eat lots of garlic, there are fewer incidences of gastric cancer, high blood pressure and high cholesterol. Dr George Lewith, Director of the Centre for the Study of Complementary Medicine, adds that garlic appears to 'boost the immune system and help fight infection by increasing the activity of immune cells'. It also has antibacterial properties from a sulphur-containing compound called allicin, formed when garlic is crushed or sliced. Cooking or processing eliminates allicin, but experts say that standardized garlic powders can form allicin when consumed. Garlic has many beneficial compounds. That's why deodorized garlic tablets and extracts seem to work as well as the raw herb in reducing cholesterol.

Who should take it? Unless you're allergic, you really can't go wrong by adding this herb to your diet. If you dislike the taste, garlic tablets will provide most of the health benefits without the flavour or odour.

E Echinacea

What it is: This flowering herb was, in great grandmother's day, found in many medicine cabinets. Echinacea [EK-in-EH-shia] fell out of favour with the introduction of antibiotics, but now it's making a comeback.

What it does: The herb has a mild protective effect against colds and flu, and in those who do fall ill it seems to limit the duration and severity of the symptoms. One study found that those with the lowest levels of white blood cells got the most benefit, which supports the theory that echinacea boosts the immune system by coaxing the body to produce more of these cells.

Who should take it? Although it doesn't work for everyone, echinacea is safe to try when you feel a cold or flu coming on. However, unless directed by a doctor, people with autoimmune disorders should avoid it. Look out for tincture or capsules, and follow label instructions And if you are allergic to flowers in the daisy family, you should be cautious.

F Zinc

What it is: An essential trace mineral. Some of the richest natural sources are shellfish and red meat.

What it does: A study at the Cleveland Clinic in America showed that after sucking on zinc lozenges, cold sufferers got better faster than those given a sugar pill. The zinc group suffered coughing, headaches and nasal congestion for four days; those who got a sugar pill stayed stuffed up for more than a week.

Who should take it? Most adults can safely take zinc lozenges to limit a cold's duration – one lozenge every four hours. Make sure the label says zinc gluconate – it is released readily into the mouth – not zinc aspartate or zinc citrate. But be cautious: too much will depress your immune system, and zinc should be avoided at daily doses above 30 milligrams.

G Omega-3 Fatty Acids

What they are: These are fats and oils essential to cardiovascular health and brain development. Sources include fish oil, flaxseed oil and green leafy vegetables.

What they do: Omega-3 fatty acids reduce the risk of cardiovascular disease by lowering triglyceride levels and blood pressure, by reducing platelet clumping that can lead to blockages and, in some cases, by lowering cholesterol. A US National Heart, Lung and Blood Institute study suggests that men who get a half gramme of these fatty acids per day can cut their risk of dying of heart disease by up to 40 per cent.

Who should take them? Everyone should include Omega-3 fatty acids in their diet, especially people with a family history of heart disease or high blood pressure. The best source is fresh fish. Ask your doctor before taking fish-oil supplements.

Paper 2 – Writing

Part 1

▶

Remember to read the instructions and texts very carefully, underlining or circling the key points.

1 You are living in an English-speaking country and, unfortunately, a number of items have been stolen from your home.

You need to write a note to your insurance company to report the burglary and request a claim form. You also need to provide a written statement for the police, describing the circumstances of the burglary, and giving details of the stolen property and any other relevant information.

Read the newspaper report on the burglary, the advertisement and the information on how to make a claim from your insurance company. Then, **using the information carefully,** write the note and statement as instructed on page 57.

▶

Avoid using words or phrases from the texts if possible. Try to express the same ideas in your own words.

NEWS in brief

Burglar Strikes

A mountain bike, worth £500, a camera, a black leather jacket and £60 in cash were stolen in a burglary at a house in High Street, Membury yesterday while the occupant was absent.

The thief forced a door to get into the house, ignoring the burglar alarm which sounded as he entered.

The bike should be easily identifiable as the frame is painted bright pink.

Car Targeted

Thieves stripped a Ford Escort of £3,000 worth of accessories at Redwood Motors in

---

Dorex The Mountain Bike Specialists

ALPINE

Climbs tall mountains, flies over bumps. Strong enough to conquer the great outdoors yet light enough to carry. Packs quickly and easily into your car boot with quick release front and rear wheels. Lightweight aluminium construction. 21 speeds.

Safe as Houses Insurance Ltd

What to do if your property is lost or stolen

1. Inform *Safe as Houses Insurance Ltd* as soon as possible.

2. Inform the police if theft is suspected.

3. Take all reasonable steps to recover the missing property.

4. Check that the loss or damage is covered by your policy.

5. Complete the claim form obtainable from the *Safe as Houses* head office.

What is covered?

Clothes and **articles** of a strictly personal nature likely to be worn, used or carried, and also **portable radios, portable TVs, sports equipment** and **bicycles.**

What is not covered?

Valuables (e.g. jewellery, watches and coin collections) or **money** (e.g. coins and bank notes, postal and money orders).

Head Office: 22 Hill Street, Bridlington, BX5 4WW

Now write:

a) a **note** to the insurance company (approximately 50 words);
b) an appropriate **statement** for the police (approximately 200 words).

You should use your own words as far as possible.

Part 2

Choose **one** of the following writing tasks. Your answer should follow exactly the instructions given. Write approximately 250 words.

▶ **Question 2**

Your report will need a main heading and also subheadings for each section (see notes on page 10). Take time to make a plan and also a list of topic vocabulary.

2 You will be working abroad for six months and have decided to reply to the following advertisement in a local newspaper.

> ### Don't leave your home empty while you're away.
> ### Let it work for you!
>
> We have clients seeking short-term accommodation
> for holidays or working visits in your area.
>
> If you would like to let your house or flat, send a full description
> (location, size, layout, equipment and any special features) together with
> details of public transport and shopping/leisure facilities nearby to:
>
> Celia Swindon, City Retreats, Exeter.

Write a **report**.

▶ **Question 3**

Notice that the company seems willing to pay you compensation so your letter should be polite but also firm. Include all the important facts and invent any extra details.

3 This is part of the letter you have received from a tour company.

> We are sorry that you were disappointed with some aspects of the travel arrangements for your recent holiday with "One World Travel" and regret that the service provided on this occasion has failed to meet our normal high standards. In order for us to investigate your complaint fully, and consider compensation, if appropriate, we should be grateful if you would send us full details of the problems you experienced.

Write a **letter**.

▶ **Question 4**

Look at the notes on page 10. As you are reviewing several items, think carefully about the organisation and headings you use.

4 An American friend of yours who speaks your language quite well has written to ask for some information and advice about newspapers in your country. He/She wants to know which ones it would be useful to read for interesting features as well as language practice. Write a review of the main newspapers in your country, describing their different characteristics, and recommend one or two which your friend might find interesting and readable.

Write the **review**.

▶ **Question 5**

Make sure you answer **both** parts of the question.

5 An international magazine is running a series of articles on the lives of young people around the world, and you have been asked to contribute a piece. Describe some of the ways in which young people in your town spend their leisure time, and suggest any improvements in the facilities that are available to them, which you would like to see in the future.

Write the **article**.

Paper 3 – English in Use

Part 1

For questions **1–15**, read the article below and then decide which word on page **60** best fits each space. Circle the letter you choose for each question. The exercise begins with an example (**0**).

Example: | 0 | D | | 0 |

Oscar's Winning Performance

Two boats, engines paralysed, are drifting (**0**) ... towards rocks in a raging sea. Gale-force winds are blowing as a distress message is relayed to the (**1**) A. . The west coast search-and-rescue helicopter takes off from Shannon; its (**2**) B. is Clew Bay in County Mayo.

The terrified crews on *Sundancer* and *Heather Berry* are only half a mile from disaster when Hotel Oscar, the Irish Marine Emergency Service helicopter arrives and the winch* crew (**3**) D saving their lives. There's no (**4**) C. for the boats – the conditions are too bad for that.

It's not easy to get the rescue line down on the rolling decks as the pilot, Captain Al Lockey hovers directly (**5**) A. . By the time the exhausted winchman has (**6**) ... the two crew members of *Heather Berry*, the helicopter is running (**7**) D. on fuel. The pair on *Sundancer* will have to be abandoned if (**8**) ... else is to survive.

For Captain Lockey, 25 years a helicopter pilot, this was the worst experience in a distinguished (**9**) ... . In fact, a change in wind direction was to (**10**) ... *Sundancer* its horrible fate, much to the (**11**) ... of the rescue crew whose hearts were breaking as they were forced to turn their backs and (**12**) C. for home. Medals, it is said, should be given to those who have to (**13**) ... that most painful decision to say 'no'. Fortunately, most crews can and (**14**) ... say 'yes' in all conditions and at all (**15**) ... of night and day.

From *Cara* magazine

*winch: a machine which is used to lift heavy objects or people who need to be rescued

0	**A** pointlessly	**B** carelessly	**C** aimlessly	**(D)** helplessly
1	**A** shore	**B** land	**C** beach	**D** seaside
2	**A** direction	**B** destination	**C** journey	**D** arrival
3	**A** set off	**B** set up	**C** set out	**D** set about
4	**A** luck	**B** way	**C** hope	**D** point
5	**A** above	**B** higher	**C** ahead	**D** over
6	**A** picked out	**B** picked up	**C** taken over	**D** taken out
7	**A** low	**B** down	**C** short	**D** out
8	**A** no one	**B** everyone	**C** someone	**D** all
9	**A** job	**B** role	**C** profession	**D** career
10	**A** spare	**B** save	**C** rescue	**D** prevent
11	**A** satisfaction	**B** comfort	**C** relief	**D** gratitude
12	**A** go	**B** fly	**C** head	**D** lead
13	**A** give	**B** do	**C** say	**D** make
14	**A** should	**B** do	**C** may	**D** need
15	**A** periods	**B** moments	**C** hours	**D** minutes

▶ **Question 10**

Three of these verbs would be followed by an object (*Sundancer*) + preposition + noun/-*ing*. Only the one that doesn't need a preposition will fit here.

▶ **Question 13**

Expressions with either *make* or *do* are often tested in the English in Use paper. It's a good idea to make a point of learning as many of these expressions as you can.

Part 2

For questions **16–30,** complete the following article by writing each missing word in the space provided. **Use only one word for each space.**
The exercise begins with an example (**0**).

Example: | 0 | by | | 0 |

Cause for Alarm?

A friend was kept awake one night recently (**0**) .... a car alarm. At 6 a.m. he stormed out and tried to force the car window open. A neighbour caught him (**16**) .... the act and (**17**) ...*instead*... of calling the police, brought out a hammer to help. (**18**) *Between*... them, they broke the window, turned off the alarm, and happily went back to bed.

The owner, (**19**) ...*when returning*... to his car, presumably thought his expensive vehicle alarm had prevented a break-in. Precisely the opposite was true. (**20**) ...*When Had*... my friend been the type who steals car radios, the alarm would have provided the perfect cover: "Stupid burglar alarms," he could have said to passers-by as he attacked the car (**21**) ...*with*... a screwdriver. So (**22**) ...*which*... is the point of alarms when everyone, (**23**) ...*apart*... from my sleepy friend, that is, ignores them?

The police, and even the manufacturers, admit (**24**) ...*so as*... much. Keith Cobham, director of Cobra Security Systems, says: "If an alarm goes off nobody (**25**) ...*will*... take any notice, even if the thief is disconnecting the batteries. The main deterrent value (**26**) ...*if*... you are the owner is that the thief does not know where *you* are."

Most alarms automatically cut out the engine, (**27**) ...*but so*... the main purpose of the noise is to deter thefts of stereos and briefcases. But as Inspector Brayne of the Metropolitan Police Crime Prevention Service points out: "This sort of theft takes place (**28**) ...*in*... split seconds. If the person (**29**) ...*has*... smashed the window, he'll carry on regardless (**30**) ...*with*... the alarm."

From *The Independent on Sunday*

▶ **Question 25**

Make sure you use the right tense. This sentence begins with *If* + present simple; what structure is that? What tense is needed here?

▶ **Question 30**

This is an example of a dependent preposition. When you learn new nouns, verbs and adjectives, make a point of learning the prepositions which go with them.

Part 3

Remember to read the **whole** text first, to get a general picture, before you check the spelling and punctuation. It's easy to miss small mistakes when you're thinking about the meaning.

In **most** lines of the following text there is either a spelling or a punctuation error. For each numbered line **31–46,** write the correctly spelled word(s) or show the correct punctuation in the space provided. Some lines are correct. Indicate these lines with a tick (✓). The exercise begins with three examples (**0**).

Examples:

0	days. It	0
0	expenses	0
0	✓	0

HOMEWORK

0   More and more people are working from home these days It

0   reduces expences and overheads to a minimum. Less time is

0   wasted on travel and there is no extra rent. Accountants need

31   little more than a desk, a calculator, some specialy ruled

32   accountancy paper and a few referrence books. Others, like

33   freelance journalists cannot manage without at least one

34   electronic or electric typewriter, fax facillities and a couple of

35   phones, plus an answering machine. Some find they cannot keep

36   up with the workload without a home computor. It needs only

37   a little imagination to convert a room into a workplace and

38   etablish instant electronic links with clients or a head office

39   hundreds' of miles away. Streamlining has become an art form

40   as manufacturers realising the need for compactness, have

41   produced space-saving equipment. Secretaries may not be

42   redundant but men and woman working from home quickly

43   realise that machines can be as eficient, if not so pleasant. Home

44   filing systems no longer need to be a bulky, four drawer cabinet.

45   An entire world of information can be stored – and retrieved –

46   in a matter of moments from a single disk hardy the size of a saucer.

▶ **Question 42**

Be careful! A word may look perfectly correct but still be spelt wrongly in the context.

31	35	39	43 ....
32	36	40	44 ....
33	37	41	45 ....
34	38	42	46 ....

Part 4

For questions **47–61** read the two texts below. Use the words in the boxes to the right of the texts, listed **47–61**, to form a word that fits in the same numbered space in the text. The exercise begins with an example (**0**).

Example: | 0 | icy | | 0 |

[handwritten: 53%]

THE FILM

On April 15th, 1912 the great ship *Titanic* sank in the (**0**) ... waters off Newfoundland with the (**47**) ... of 1,523 lives. The (**48**) ... of the ship on its maiden voyage from Southampton to New York is the most (**49**) ... ocean disaster of all time, and a tragedy that has had an unparalleled hold over our collective (**50**) ... . Interest in the wreck, and the powerful human stories of the (**51**) ... has never waned. Quite the opposite. And in 1998, the world's (**52**) ... with the story was further fuelled by the release of James Cameron's film *Titanic*, which broke all box-office records to become the most successful film in cinema history, with (**53**) ... takings of $1.8 billion.

(0)	ICE
(47)	LOSE *[handwritten: lost ✗]*
(48)	SINK *[handwritten: sank ✗]*
(49)	LEGEND *[handwritten: legendary / ary ✓]*
(50)	CONSCIOUS *[handwritten: ✗ consciousness]*
(51)	SURVIVE *[handwritten: survivors ✓]*
(52)	FASCINATE *[handwritten: -tion ✗]*
(53)	GLOBE *[handwritten: global ✓]*

[handwritten margin: 3]

▶ Question 51

This refers to the **people** who survived the shipwreck, so you need to use a plural.

THE DIRECTOR

If all the stories about the Canadian director of the film *Titanic*, James Cameron, were true, only a fool would want to spend an hour in his company, for fear of great personal injury or an (**54**) ... mugging. But he is (**55**) ... charming and (**56**) ... when you meet him. Cameron, a university drop-out who worked as a machinist and a truck driver before following his (**57**) ... obsession into films, does not worry about the myths that surround him. But, (**58**) ... he is aware that he is regarded as a (**59**) ... autocrat? "That is always written by people who have never met me," he says. "Journalists don't see the (**60**) ... and intimate (**61**) ... I have with actors. I have never yelled at an actor in my entire career."

(54)	EMOTION *[handwritten: -al ✓]*
(55)	SURPRISE *[handwritten: singly ✓]*
(56)	COURTESY *[handwritten: courteous ✗]*
(57)	CHILD *[handwritten: -hood ✓]*
(58)	SURE *[handwritten: -ly ✓]*
(59)	SPECTACLE *[handwritten: spectacular ✗]*
(60)	CREATE *[handwritten: creativity ✗]*
(61)	RELATION *[handwritten: -ship ✓]*

▶ Question 55

What part of speech qualifies an adjective (*charming*)? Form the adjective first and then add a suitable suffix.

---

47	52	57 ....
48	53	58 ....
49	54	59 ....
50	55	60 ....
51	56	61 ....

Part 5

▶

Remember your answers
must fit the text
grammatically **and**
stylistically.

For questions **62–74,** read the following informal note about a magazine
competition and use the information to complete the numbered gaps in the formal
announcement. **Use no more than two words** for each gap. The words you need **do
not occur** in the informal note. The exercise begins with an example (**0**).

Example: | 0 | or more | | 0 |

INFORMAL NOTE

Dear Carl,

How about organising a photography competition for
the magazine? We could get a few people who are well-
known in the field to decide on the best shots. I'm
sure Mary Thorpe would agree to help, for example
– she's a friend of my mother's. As 1st prize, we could
offer a copy of that new camera manual we were sent
and maybe some useful equipment (say twenty pounds'
worth?) for the 2nd prize.

If you agree, let's print an official entry form – so
people have to buy the magazine! There could be several
categories but I think we should set a limit for each
entrant of three photos altogether, however many
categories they enter. You'll need to decide when entries
have to be in by, and what the smallest size for prints
should be. Tell people to send a SAE of the right size if
they want their photos back, and add a note to say they
can't blame us (or claim compensation) if anything
happens to their photographs. We could put the results
(and some of the best pictures?) in a future edition.

Mandy

FORMAL ANNOUNCEMENT

PHOTOGRAPHY COMPETITION

Entries are invited for the **Photograph of the Year** competition for one (0) .... of the following THREE categories:

1. Town   2. Countryside   3. Wildlife

Entries will be (62) .... , by a panel of (63) .... , including Mary Thorpe, editor of 'You and Your Camera', and the best photographs will (64) .... in next month's magazine.

- **First Prize:** 'Complete Guide to Photography' by Martin Webber.

- **Second Prize:** Camera equipment to the (65) .... of £20.

RULES

1) Entrants may submit no more than three photographs in (66) ....

2) Photographs can be in colour or black and white and must be of a (67) .... size: 10 cm x 14 cm.

3) All entrants (68) .... the official entry form printed on page 26.

4) The (69) .... for entries is 31st December.

5) Photographs cannot be (70) .... unless they are (71) .... by a stamped addressed envelope of (72) .... size.

6) Prize-winners will be (73) .... in next month's magazine.

7) No (74) .... can be taken for any loss or damage to photographs.

▶ **Question 70**

Remember you can't use words from the first text. You need a slightly more formal expression here.

Part 6

For questions **75–80**, read through the following text and then choose from the list **A–J** the best phrase given below it to fill each of the spaces. Write one letter (**A–J**) in each space provided. **Some of the suggested answers do not fit at all.** The exercise begins with an example (**0**).

Example: 0 J  0

> **▶ Question 75**
>
> Sentence 75 links with the next section. There's a clue in the word *suburbs*.

> **▶ Question 79**
>
> Sentence 79 provides a contrast to the previous one. The point is explained in more detail in the sentence which follows.

CAR CHAOS

On the surface, Los Angeles seems to be an extremely convenient city. With hundreds of miles of freeways criss-crossing the city, cars can move around two or three times faster than in European cities like London. (0) ... This is because "Angelinos" also have to travel three times as far. Speed is not much of an advantage when the additional distance you have to travel soaks up the time you gain.

Although LA has the second largest bus fleet in the US, only three per cent of journeys are made by bus. (75) ... It's almost impossible to live without a car in the "drive-in" suburbs. (76) ... How would you get to the bank, the school or the office? The answer is obvious. You drive because things are so spread out that you can't do anything else. In the inner city, there is less mobility. (77) ... Many cannot drive. Others cannot afford a car. And, in any case, driving is unpleasant because of the congestion. Public transport is expensive, unless it is subsidized. (78) ...

The inner cities tend to be the older and more historic parts. They are now being violently disrupted to make them fit for cars. In this process people are being edged out and treated as second-class citizens. (79) ...

It is no accident that cars should have dominated North American and Australian cities so completely. (80) ... Not just for motorways but also for parking, whether at home, in the city centre for office workers or by the supermarket for shoppers.

From *The New Internationalist*

A And the poor can't afford high fares.

B Los Angeles has around half this figure.

C The car gets first-class treatment.

D Driving is as natural as breathing; to be carless would be almost un-American.

E Cars need vast tracts of land.

F Some are old and have never learnt to drive.

G Outside the denser inner area, bus services barely exist.

H But it is not unique.

I Here the people rely on public transport.

J But the *impression* of speed is all it is.

Paper 4 – Listening

Part 1

You will hear part of a radio programme about answering machines. For questions **1–9**, fill in the missing information.

You will hear the recording twice.

Answering machines usually limit the length of | **1**
you make.

Most models also limit the time available to

| **2**

Most models allow you to listen to your messages from

| **3**

Two-way recording of conversations may be useful if you use your phone

| **4**

Overall, the **Budgie** answering machine was considered basic but

| **5**

The **Cuckoo** can be wall-mounted, which is a useful way of

| **6**

Although it worked well, the method for dealing with messages was

| **7**

The **Vulture** was very easy to use and the recordings were

| **8**

However, overall it was considered | **9**

▶ **Question 6**

Remember that the recording may use slightly different words from the question. Think of another way of saying *wall-mounted*.

67

Part 2

You will hear a tour guide giving a group of tourists some extra details about their programme. As you listen, complete the information for questions **10–17**.

Listen very carefully as you will hear the recording ONCE only.

Sunday September 14th

Arrive at Amman and transfer to your hotel.

p.m.   ~~Welcome dinner~~   Hotel will provide [_____] **10**
and fruit.

Monday September 15th

a.m.   Breakfast   Served beside [_____] **11**
Coach tour of city

p.m.   Free   Optional visit to [_____] **12**
Buffet dinner with [_____] **13**

Tuesday September 16th

a.m.   Breakfast   Remember to wear [_____] **14**

Coaches depart for Petra   Journey takes [_____] **15**
Tour of ancient city followed
by lunch at Petra Vista Hotel

p.m.   Depart Petra   Coach leaves at [_____] **16**
Stop at Turkish fort for [_____] **17**

1001 Arabian Nights Dinner

▶ **Questions 11 and 12**

You can use note answers, for example omitting the definite article.

▶ **Question 16**

You can use the shortest forms, e.g. numbers instead of words, and *p.m.* instead of *o'clock*.

Part 3

You will hear an interview with a subeditor on a newspaper.
For questions **18–24,** choose the correct option from **A, B, C** or **D.**

You will hear the recording twice.

▶

With multiple choice
questions, read through
all the questions first, if
possible, and try to
predict the correct
answers.

18 He only works on *The Australian* part-time because
    A there's no full-time work available.
    B he also works on another newspaper.
    C he prefers not to work full-time.
    D he's still learning about the job.

19 Part of his work involves
    A writing new articles.
    B correcting mistakes.
    C training new reporters.
    D choosing pictures for articles.

20 Why are 'breakout heads' used?
    A To fill up space on the page.
    B To attract the reader's attention.
    C To explain what is shown in the pictures.
    D To make the page look more readable.

21 How has his work changed in recent years?
    A He has to start work earlier.
    B He has to write for other newspapers.
    C There are more editions to prepare.
    D There is more overseas material.

22 One problem the newspaper has is that
    A it doesn't have any new technology.
    B it doesn't have the latest technology.
    C editors refuse to use new technology.
    D editors aren't trained to use new technology.

23 'House ads' advertise different
    A business opportunities.
    B types of accommodation.
    C sections of the newspaper.
    D newspapers in the same group.

24 What seems to be his opinion of his newspaper's attitude to headlines?
    A A bit too serious.
    B In bad taste.
    C Rather dishonest.
    D Admirable.

Part 4

You will hear five short extracts in which various people are talking about publications they read.

Remember that the answer may not be directly stated on the tape. Listen for clues in what the speakers say about the publications they read.

TASK ONE

For questions **25–29,** match the extracts as you hear them with the publications the speakers read, listed **A–H.**

A a local newspaper

B a national daily newspaper

C a children's comic

D a music magazine

E a trade or professional journal

F a TV guide

G a satirical magazine

H a Sunday newspaper

A	25
E	26
H	27
D	28
A	29

TASK TWO

For questions **30–34,** match the extracts as you hear them with the speakers' favourite features, listed **A–H.**

The speakers may not use the exact words in the questions. Listen for abbreviations or other ways of referring to the features listed.

A critics' reviews

B lonely hearts column

C detailed news reports

D competitions

E advertisements

F sports reports

G readers' letters

H horoscope

	30
E	31
	32
	33
F	34

**Remember that you must complete both tasks as you listen.
You will hear the recording twice.**

Paper 5 – Speaking

Work with another student.

Part 1 (3 minutes) Introductions and General Social Conversation

▶

Remember to ask these questions in your own words, as naturally as possible.

Really listen to what your partner has to say and ask some follow-up questions, if possible.

Imagine you had never met your partner.

- Introduce yourselves to each other.

- Find out where your partner lives and how he/she feels about that place. Give your partner the same information about yourself.

- Tell your partner about a good friend of yours. Ask your partner about his/her friends.

- Find out what kind of physical exercise your partner takes. Explain what exercise you take.

Part 2 (3 or 4 minutes)

▶

Remember that each candidate should aim to talk for about **a minute,** without interruptions.

There are three main parts to the instructions. Make sure you do everything you are asked to.

In this part of the test you will each have the opportunity to talk for a minute.

Tasks 1 and 2

Places of Work (Describe, hypothesise and contrast)

You will each see a picture showing someone's place of work and you must talk to your partner about the room and its occupant, saying what you think the picture tells you about the person's working life, and whether it appeals to you or not.

Let your partner see your picture while you're talking.

You each have about one minute for this.

When you've finished talking about your picture, you can comment on each other's observations and decide which is the best working environment.

Candidate A: Turn to the picture on page 148 and talk about your picture.

Candidate B: Turn to the picture on page 146.

Now look at each other's pictures again and see if you agree or disagree with what has already been said. Which picture shows the best working environment?

You have about a minute for this.

Part 3 (3 or 4 minutes)

Pick a Prize (Evaluate and select)

In this part of the test you have to discuss a topic with your partner.

You have both won a competition run by a company which specialises in new and slightly unusual products. As a prize, you can choose any of the items from the company's catalogue shown on page 147.

Discuss with your partner how useful you consider each item to be. Explain which one you would choose as your prize. It could be for yourself, as a present for a friend, or even as a present for someone you don't like! Find out what your partner would choose, and why.

You have three or four minutes for this.

▶

Remember to give your partner an equal opportunity to speak, and to listen carefully to what he/she says.

Part 4 (3 or 4 minutes)

In this part of the test you and your partner have to report on the outcome of your discussion in Part 3, saying whether you agreed or not. You then take part in a more general discussion with your partner and the examiner.

Practise your reporting and discussion skills by working with another pair. Take it in turns to summarise and explain the conclusions you reached, and then discuss the following questions:

▶

You'll need to summarise your discussion and explain the reasons for your decisions.

- What are the advantages and disadvantages of buying by mail order?
- Which family members are most difficult to buy presents for? Why?
- Do you think it's acceptable to give money instead of a present?
- Is it more enjoyable to give a present or to receive one?

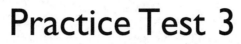

Practice Test 3
Paper 1 – Reading

Part 1

Answer questions **1–17** by referring to the article on children's competitions on page **74**.

For questions **1–17** answer by choosing from the sections of the article (**A–J**) printed on page 74. Some of the choices may be required more than once.

Note: When more than one answer is required, these may be given **in any order**.

For which competition or competitions do you have to

buy some food? **1** ....

open a building society account? **2** .... **3** ....

phone for information? **4** ....

watch television? **5** ....

go to a post office? **6** ....

In which competition or competitions could you win

a holiday abroad? **7** .... **8** ....

a book? **9** ....

sweets? **10** ....

make-up? **11** ....

money? **12** ....

a trip to a sports event? **13** ....

Which competition or competitions would be suitable for

animal lovers? **14** ....

artistic children? **15** .... **16** .... **17** ....

▶ **Questions 10 and 11**

Like many of these questions, 10 and 11 use general terms. You need to look for specific examples in the text.

▶ **Paragraph J**

If you don't know a word (like *chimp*), look for any extra information in the text which might help explain the meaning.

How to win prizes for keeping quiet

Finding it difficult to keep the children amused during the long, dark evenings? The answer, **Jane Bidder** says, is to get them hooked on competitions.

The chance of winning something for nothing, apart from a little know-how, is always attractive, and provides an opportunity for children to prove their artistic or verbal skills. Below (with the help of my three children), I have tracked down the most exciting competitions for tinies through to teenagers.

A **Good writers** can show off their calligraphic skills with the Osmiroid Spirit of the Letter Competition, run by Berol. There are four entry classes, from designing a small poster to producing a notice for a nature trail. Prizes include a calligraphic weekend and equipment. Closing date May 31 1993. Age ten upwards. Entry forms from Berol, Oldmeadow Road, Kings Lynn, Norfolk PE30 4JR.

B **Babies** too young for most competitions can pose for a photograph to enter Mothercare's happy faces competition in either the 0–18 months category, or 18 months to five years. Running in selected stores throughout Britain, the competition prizes include a family holiday for four to Euro Disney in Paris, video camcorders and vouchers. Ring Paintbox Portraits on 0722 412202 to find your nearest store competition.

C **Colour** a pantomime scene in Snap magazine (December issue) and win a Sega Master system, or one of 20 mystery Christmas stockings for runners-up (closing date December 14). Or, in the same issue, answer a simple question about a children's illustrator and win one of 20 chocolate selection stockings plus party tapes. Or again, complete a sentence about Disney's *Basil the Great Mouse Detective* and win one of five videos. Closing date for these two competitions is December 20.

D **Canny comp:** Enter the Heinz Spaghetti competition by filling in the prize draw form (inside the label) to win one of 1,000 Sega Master Systems II (are we the only family not to have one?). Closing date November 27.

> *What better confidence booster than for a child to be able to cry, 'I've won'?*

E **Young writers:** Look out for the Royal Mail Young Letter Writer competition – leaflets available in most post offices at the beginning of January. The theme is still to be decided: last year's subject was anything 'green'. Prizes range from £100 for regional winners to £400 for national winners. Closing date: first week in April.

F **Family holiday:** Parents would be delighted if a child won a week's holiday in Boston, USA, for a family of four – the first prize in Harrods' Freedom Trail in-store competition. The competition starts on December 14, when Father Christmas arrives (free admission to grotto) and ends December 24. Entrants (under the age of 12) have to answer questions on New England landmarks.

G **Camera caper:** Prove your photographic skills by taking a photograph (with your own camera or someone else's) and win a trip to the Wimbledon tennis next summer by joining the Halifax Building Society LittleXtra Club. Other competitions, detailed in the free club magazine, include identifying three road signs to win a Corgi garage, and completing a puzzle to pocket one of 30 *Where's Wally?* videos. Open to children under 11. Closing date for all entries is March 29. Children can join the club at any Halifax branch by opening an account.

H **Scribble a few lines** about yourself and send in your picture to *Mandy & Judy* comic for its Reader of the Week competition. The winner receives a range of Polly Pocket Pretty Me cosmetics.

I **Under six year olds** can design a Christmas picture in any medium and win Bluebird toys, including Jumbo Fun Plane, Big Red Fun Bus, Big Yellow Teapot, with teasets and lunchboxes for runners up. Watch Children's Channel on satellite/cable TV (8.45–10.45am and 1–3pm).

J **Adopt a chimp** by answering a true/false question about chimpanzees in the Woolwich Building Society's Kids Club magazine (details below). You can then be the official adoptive owner of a four-legged pet at the Chimp Rescue Centre in Wareham, Dorset. Less zoo-minded readers might prefer tamer prizes from the Woolwich, such as *The Guinness Book of Records* (answer multiple choice questions) or a board game (spot the odd one out). Entry forms are in the company magazine, which is sent to you after opening an account for £1. Under-12s only.

Part 2

For questions **18–23** you must choose which of the paragraphs **A–G** on page **76** fit into the numbered gaps in the following newspaper article. There is one extra paragraph which does not fit in any of the gaps.

Prince of Whales

By Robin Eggar

Once hunted to the edge of extinction, the sperm whale is bringing new life to an ocean community which preyed on them.

The history of Kaikoura, on New Zealand's South Island, is inextricably bound with that of the whale. It owes its very creation and continuing existence to these beautiful creatures. The town was built on slaughtered whales; on whale-bone, blubber and sperm oil – and nearly died with the creatures it preyed on.

18

Whaling lingered on – in 1963, 248 sperm whales were killed – until the bottom fell out of the market. In 1978, New Zealand outlawed the killing of any marine mammal, whales, dolphins and seals, in her waters.

19

In 1988, local fisherman Roger Sutherland, his American wife Barbara Todd and the Maori-financed Kaikoura Tours started to explore the commercial viability of whale watching. In just four years the whole atmosphere of the town has been transformed. Now the very creature Kaikoura preyed on has given it a new lease of life. For it is the only place on earth where one can watch sperm whales so close at hand. Where once the boats sailed forth to kill, they now ferry out the tourists to marvel, watch and wonder.

20

The seas around Kaikoura are a marine wonderland, teeming with crayfish and groper, and colonies of seals. On this planet there are 76 species of whale and dolphin, 15 of which can be seen regularly in Kaikoura waters.

21

While young males tend to move about individually or in pairs, lucky visitors occasionally see something special. "I had 15 whales all in a line for about 15 minutes once," says Richard Oliver, Kaikoura sea operations manager and expert at locating whales with a hydrophone (underwater microphone). Although some whales can be playful, they generally stay aloof. "They tolerate us for their own pleasure and perhaps curiosity," says Richard. "They have minds of their own, different temperaments and there are a couple I completely trust. Being out there on the ocean with them is an awe-inspiring thing."

22

An unknown author once wrote: Whatever that ancient chemistry of gentle change that produced great whales, it will never again be duplicated in the lifetime of this planet. If we allow the extinction of whales, we and they will never have another chance.

23

▶ **Question 21**

The section before talks about how many species can be seen. The missing section refers to this and also has a direct link with the next paragraph.

▶ **Question 19**

There are two clues, one in the section before: *In 1978 ...* and one in the section following: *Roger Sutherland ...* . Look for a paragraph which links these two points.

A   Although primarily appealing to young, backpacking eco-tourists, whale watching has caught the public imagination. Last year 40,000 people took the £27 three-hour trip, with a subsequent knock-on effect for the local economy. Hotel occupancy is up from 15 per cent to 96 per cent in four years, while property prices are rising faster than anywhere in New Zealand.

B   Perhaps they are better at forgiveness than we are. Playful humpback whales are returning to Kaikoura waters. Absent for the past 25 years, they have been sighted in increasing numbers for the past two Julys. But it may not be enough. Some nations have chosen to abandon the international ban on commercial whaling and so threaten the world's whales.

C   The whales have given the town of Kaikoura another chance. Surely, we owe them the same?

D   By then the whales had long been forgotten, except in the folk memory of fishermen and Maori story-tellers. Kaikoura slid into slow, seemingly irreversible decline. Until someone remembered the whales.

E   As the whale sinks into the trough between the waves, he exhales a snow-white spray from his blow-hole. For 10 minutes the ritual continues until, accompanied by sighs of disappointment, the body vanishes beneath the water.

F   This remarkable abundance is all down to a trick of geology and geography. Less than a mile offshore the continental shelf drops into deep-water canyons just where a warm southbound current converges with a cold northerly one. This produces a thriving food chain and ideal conditions for young male sperm whales, who spend their adolescent years, from 13 to 25, there until they are mature enough to breed.

G   Maori legend tells of Paikea who first rode into South Bay on the back of Tohora, a giant whale. Then came the pakeha (white man) with their harpoons, men like Scot George Fyffe who established a whaling station in 1842. When it closed 80 years later, the whales were close to extinct.

Part 3

Read the following newspaper article and then answer questions **24–29** on page **78**.
Indicate the letter **A**, **B**, **C** or **D** against the number of each question **24–29**.
Give only one answer to each question.

Classrooms with the writing on the wall

Maintaining classroom discipline is a growing problem for many schools. Some children seem incapable of following the rules, perhaps because they feel they are unreasonable or unclear.

There can be no such excuses at Bebington High School on the Wirral. When children misbehave at Bebington, the teacher immediately writes their names on the classroom blackboard. They know they are in trouble and they know what the penalty is likely to be. Their classmates know too that the choice to break the rules was their own.

The effect, claim the proponents of this American system of discipline, has been to improve behaviour, allowing more time to be spent on teaching. "Assertive discipline" was introduced into Bebington last September and Margaret Hodson, a science teacher, says the results are "little short of a miracle".

Since the programme was introduced into England two years ago, 450 schools, 80 per cent of them primary have adopted the scheme. Whether the programme spreads more widely depends to some extent on the government's attitude. Adrian Smith, of Behaviour Management, the Bristol-based company marketing the scheme in Britain, will this week meet Eric Forth, the Junior Schools Minister, to tell him of the benefits achieved by schools using the programme.

Bebington, a 1,000-pupil 11-to-18 secondary modern school, was always considered good for a school of its type, but staff claim that standards of behaviour increased dramatically last term, with an improvement in the work rate of the children and less stress on the teachers.

The basis of the programme, which costs schools £22 a day for each person trained, is that all children have a right to choose how they behave but they must face the consequences of that choice. A set of straightforward rules is displayed on a wall in each classroom, together with a set of rewards and consequences.

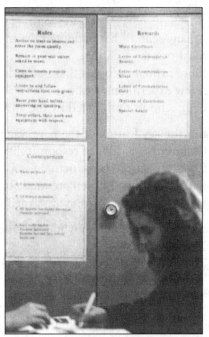

No excuses: Lesley Ann McFeat at work at Bebington

The rules at Bebington are: arrive on time to lessons and enter the room quietly; remain in your seat unless asked to move; come to lessons properly equipped; listen to and follow instructions the first time they are given; raise your hand before answering or speaking; and treat others, their work and equipment with respect.

Pupils who behave well during a lesson are rewarded with an "R" mark in the teacher's record book. Six Rs win them a "bronze" letter of commendation to take home to their parents. Twelve "Rs" bring a silver letter, 18 a gold, and 24 a diploma of excellence presented by the head teacher at assembly. Diploma winners are then able to choose a special award in negotiation with staff, such as a non-uniform day or a trip out.

Teachers can also award a certificate of merit for individual pieces of good work or behaviour or for long-term excellent punctuality or attendance. All letters and certificates earned by the pupils are eventually kept in their record of achievement, available to potential employers.

The sanctions open to teachers for pupils who break the rules are: detention of five minutes, 15 minutes or 30 minutes at lunchtime with the parents informed. The ultimate sanction before being excluded is being sent to the academic remove, where children are isolated from the rest of the school for periods ranging from one lesson to a whole day. They are continually supervised by a member of the staff and their parents are invited to the school to discuss their child's behaviour.

Assertive discipline allows the staff to deal quickly with disruptive pupils: children can see the consequence of their action on the wall. As a result, the time spent on teaching in the classroom is up substantially, says John Adamson, a modern languages teacher at the school.

In adapting the scheme for British use, the Bebington staff, who all agreed that it was the right move for their school, had to revise the rewards system, which in American schools tends to be material. Offers of sweets or gifts for good behaviour were deemed inappropriate.

Paul Shryane, the deputy head at Bebington, says: "Much assertive discipline is based on sound traditional educational practice. What is new is the formalised consistency of a whole school approach, and the consistent rewarding of those who achieve the standards asked of them."

Put rather more controversially, society has moved on, it seems, from the time where the teacher could expect good behaviour from the majority of pupils as a matter of course. Now they have to reward it.

DAVID TYTLER

24 What are the results of the new system at Bebington High School?
   A It's too early to say.
   B Disappointing so far.
   C Fairly promising.
   D Very encouraging.

25 How many schools have adopted the new scheme?
   A Most primary schools.
   B More primary schools than secondary schools.
   C A few experimental schools.
   D Only schools nominated by the government.

> **▶ Question 26**
>
> Option **D**: Beware of options which contain words which are the same as, or similar to, words in the text. They may not mean exactly the same thing.

26 What is the key feature of the new system?
   A Children learn to take responsibility for their actions.
   B Children have to be punctual for all their lessons.
   C Badly-behaved children are made to feel ashamed.
   D Well-behaved children are awarded with medals.

27 What happens to children who continue to behave badly?
   A They are sent home.
   B Their parents are asked to discipline them.
   C They are kept away from other pupils for a time.
   D They have to miss lunch.

> **▶ Question 28**
>
> Option **D**: Beware of 'all-or-nothing' options which may say more than is actually true.

28 How does the scheme in Britain compare with the American one?
   A The rules are stricter.
   B The punishments are less severe.
   C The rewards are different.
   D It's exactly the same.

29 What seems to be the writer's view of the subject?
   A The system is more suitable for America than Britain.
   B It's a pity good behaviour can't be taken for granted any more.
   C Children who behave badly should be helped, not punished.
   D It's a controversial idea and only time will tell if it's successful.

Part 4

Answer questions **30–49** by referring to the newspaper article about cruising on pages **80–81**.

For questions **30–49** choose your answer from the list of ships (**A–E**). Some choices may be required more than once.

Note: When more than one answer is required, these may be given **in any order**.

▶ Questions 30–35

These are rapid skimming questions. You can find the information at the beginning of each section. Don't read any further at this stage.

Which ship was built most recently?	**30**	
Which ship has the largest crew?	**31**	
Which ship has the fewest passengers?	**32**	
Which is the biggest ship?	**33**	
Which cruise lasts longest?	**34**	
Which cruise has the cheapest fare?	**35**	

A Norway

Which cruise would be most suitable for

▶ Questions 36–42

Look out for different ways of expressing these ideas in the text.

older people?	**36**	**37**.........
people with children?	**38**	
people interested in photography?	**39**	
people interested in golf?	**40**	
people interested in shopping?	**41**	**42** ....

B Queen Elizabeth II

C Royal Princess

D Royal Viking Sun

Which ship was considered most comfortable to travel in?	**43**	
Which ship has an excellent library?	**44**	
On which cruise were the tours specially recommended?	**45**	
On which cruise are you likely to see whales?	**46**	**47** ....
Which cruise had the best entertainment?	**48**	
Which cruise had the worst restaurant service?	**49**	

E Sagafjord

Cruising

COMPARING THE OPTIONS

Our aim was to compare facilities, styles, route and prices on a variety of cruises. We award marks out of 10.

THE BIG SHIPS

A NORWAY: *1,035ft long; 75,000 tons; 2,044 passengers; built 1961. Norwegian officers, international crew (800 in total). Cruise: Caribbean (Miami–Miami;) 7 days. £965–£3,485.*

They don't come any bigger. Always the longest and, after a recent refit, the heaviest, but mercifully not the most passenger-intensive. It's easy to get lost among three-football-pitch-long corridors; if you forget your sunglasses it could be a 10-minute hike back to the cabin.

There are 12 cabin categories, all bright and cheerful, including four-berth family versions. This is an ideal family cruise, with lots of activities for toddlers and teenagers, and big discounts. Adult entertainment includes Las Vegas-style evening shows.

Dining is in two restaurants, or queues for hamburgers 'n' fries on deck.

The route is standard Caribbean. Lots of shopping at St John's, St Thomas and St Maarten, swimming and barbecuing on Norwegian Cruise Line's private Bahamian island.

Rating: cabins 8; service 8; food 2; entertainment 10; excursions 5; route 2. **Atmosphere:** youngish, American, families.

B QUEEN ELIZABETH II: *963ft long; 66,451 tons; 1,870 passengers; built 1969. Officers: British; crew: British/international (1,015). Cruise: Transatlantic (Southampton–New York); 5 days (each way). £1,100–£2,430 (both ways).*

Unless you are exceptionally lucky, this won't be a sunshine cruise but the ship is well-prepared to amuse her customers in bad weather, with two indoor swimming pools as well as three on deck, a shopping concourse featuring Harrods, Burberry and Aquascutum, good lectures, heavy leather armchairs and the best ship's library afloat.

Cabins vary enormously, with 22 grades. It's important to realise that the dining goes with the cabin grade. Only the very top get to the admirable Princess and Queen's Grills; the so-called "First Class" get the Columbia restaurant and the rest mass catering in the Mauretania.

Rating: cabins 2–8 depending on grade; service 7; food 4–10 depending on grade; entertainment 8; lectures 9. **Atmosphere:** stately as a galleon. **High spot:** arrival in New York.

THE MEDIUM SHIPS

C ROYAL PRINCESS: *761ft long, 44,348 tons, 1,260 passengers, built 1984. British officers, international crew (500). Cruise: The Northern Capitals (The Baltic Sea); 12 days. £1,745–£4,920.*

An easy ship to find your way around. I particularly liked the deck area, with a choice of three swimming pools and four spa baths.

All cabins are well fitted, most have baths and are outside; those with verandahs are as splendid as any afloat. The interior features attractive paintings from a well-chosen modern art collection.

Lectures are well-researched and there was a commentary from the captain during the most interesting passages, and for whale-spotting. Dinner is better than most mass catering and the breakfast and lunch buffets are outstanding.

The Baltic is a popular cruising ground and for a whistle-stop tour of some of the most interesting cities in Europe, it's hard to beat. Good tours were arranged in every port but none of them is essential unless you can't use your legs.

Rating: cabins 5–9; service 8; food 5 in dining room, 8 in buffet; entertainment 9; route 10. **Atmosphere:** jolly, middle-aged. **High spots:** Copenhagen, Stockholm, St Petersburg, Amsterdam.

D ROYAL VIKING SUN: *673ft long; 36,845 tons, 740 passengers; built 1972. Norwegian officers, Scandinavian crew (460). Cruise: New York, New England, St Lawrence river to Montreal and back to New York; 14 days. £2,271 (inside cabin) to £7,300 (suite).*

This is a ship unique in combining luxury with considerable size. If you come into this spending bracket, you can hardly fault her. She is certainly the smoothest, quietest ship I sampled, the food in the dining room, and particularly in the Garden Room Buffet, is outstanding, and the public rooms are spacious and comfortable. All the cabins have walk-in cupboards and full-size bathrooms, many have verandahs: you could be in a very exclusive hotel.

Deck space is generous – no need to reserve your space before breakfast – and you can actually do more than three strokes at a time in the swimming pool (very unusual). A unique feature is the golf simulator where a professional gives advice on shots directed at a screen.

The Sun is a very popular ship and aims to please all tastes. There are classical music concerts and also bingo and a casino; evening entertainment and lectures were disappointing.

Rating: cabins 9; service 10; food 9 for restaurant, 10 for buffet; entertainment 4; excursions 5. **Atmosphere:** sophisticated. **High spots:** Boston, Quebec, Montreal, Newport.

E SAGAFJORD: *619ft long; 24,474 tons; 620 passengers; built 1965. Norwegian officers, international crew (350). Cruise: Alaska (Vancouver to Anchorage); 13 days. £2,195 inside double, to £6,840 for penthouse suite.*

This is the second most popular cruise route in the world and the long cruise is more than justified by the never-failing excitement of scenery and wildlife. Leave the deck and binoculars for a meal, or to fetch sunglasses (you'll need them), and you miss a bear, a whale, a glacier and another stupendous photo-opportunity.

Cabins are pleasantly pastel, mostly with baths, and there is the obligatory gym and sauna. Cold weather provisions include an indoor swimming pool and lots of blankets to wrap round frozen legs. A unique feature is the local retired ladies who give daily lectures on their home grounds. Our lecture was better and more inspiring than most given by professionals.

This is one route where excursions are essential. There are 64 options. To go so far and miss the helicopter landing on the glacier or the White Pass railway ride into the Yukon would be a shame.

Rating: cabins 8; service 2 in dining room and decks (long waits, poor wine service), 8 in cabins; food: 5 restaurant, 7 Lido buffet; entertainment 5; lectures 10; route 10. **Atmosphere:** enthusiastic, middle-aged. **High spots:** Hubbard and College glaciers.

Paper 2 – Writing

Part I

There's a lot of information to digest here so it's **very** important to highlight the key points.

1 You are planning to spend two weeks in Sydney, Australia, attending a conference, and a friend has sent you a brochure for a company which rents apartments there.

You have decided to write to the rental company explaining what type of accommodation you are interested in and when you require it, and asking for the extra information you need. You also want to write to your friend, thanking them for the information, and telling them briefly what you have done.

Read the brochure and the notes you have made on it and the extract from your friend's letter. Then, **using the information carefully,** write the letter and note as instructed on page 83.

★★ STAR POINT ★★
HOLIDAY APARTMENTS
For excellent short-term accommodation

(weekly rates?)

With apartments in most areas of Sydney, we can place you close to friends or family or just minutes away from the main business or tourist districts. Tell us the reason for your visit, and we'll make sure you're conveniently located.

All apartments are completely self-contained and furnished to a high standard. They are fully equipped with colour television, linen, crockery and kitchen needs.

iron?
hairdryer?
laundry facilities?

Each apartment has a telephone and **all your local calls are free of charge!**

How are international calls charged?

Bookings are flexible. Rent on a daily, weekly or monthly basis. Apartments without a harbour view are available at lower rates.

What is this exactly?

Example Rental Fees (Daily)

Apartment Category	Harbour View	Other Outlook
Studio	$65-75	$55-65
1 Bedroom	$75-85	$65-75
2 Bedroom	$95-105	$85-95

(deposit required?)

WE WILL NEED TO KNOW

- The dates of your arrival and departure — (10-25 Aug)
- How many people will be staying
- How large an apartment you need
- Which area of the city you would prefer — (near Bondi Beach if poss.)

I enclose a brochure for rented apartments which I picked up when I was in Sydney last (the prices may be slightly out of date now). I imagine weekly rates are cheaper than the daily ones quoted. As you're on your own, you could opt for a "Studio" (a kind of bed-sitter, I suppose) and I'm sure you could manage without a harbour view. It would be much nicer to have your own apartment, and you'd save a lot by cooking for yourself rather than eating out. Why not write to the company and check a few details? Let me know how you get on.

Jan

▶

Make sure you answer **both** parts of the question – you'll lose a lot of marks if you don't write the note.

Now write:

a) a **letter of enquiry** to the rental company (approximately 200 words);
b) a **note** to your friend (approximately 50 words).

You should use your own words as far as possible.

Part 2

Choose **one** of the following writing tasks. Your answer should follow exactly the instructions given. Write approximately 250 words.

▶ **Question 2**

Think carefully about the layout and style. See guidelines for writing a leaflet on page 9.

2   You work for a travel company which is organising Fly/Drive holidays to your country for British tourists. You have been asked to prepare a leaflet giving general information about the different regions of the country, suggesting one or two routes drivers could take, and mentioning any places particularly worth visiting.

Write the text for the **leaflet**.

▶ **Question 3**

Notice that you don't necessarily think that Michael Brown is totally wrong in his views. Your article should aim to offer a more balanced argument.

3   This letter appeared in a magazine. You think the writer has exaggerated the problems and failed to mention some worthwhile programmes. Write an article expressing your views.

> Sir,
>
> Why is television so awful these days? I look in vain for anything of educational value, originality or genuine artistic merit. I'm afraid to let my children watch television alone for fear of the damaging effect some of the more violent dramas may have on them. I have now decided to get rid of our TV, and I suggest other readers do the same.
>
> Yours faithfully,
>
> **MICHAEL BROWN**

Write the **article** for the magazine.

▶ **Question 4**

Remember to organise your report clearly, with suitable headings (see notes on page 10).

4   The international company you work for sent you on a two-week English course recently. In order to decide whether to send more employees to the same centre in future, the company has asked you to write a report, commenting on the course content, the teaching and the social programme, saying whether you feel you derived any benefit from the course, and making any recommendations you feel are appropriate.

Write your **report**.

▶ **Question 5**

This is an opportunity to tell an interesting story. The application can be in the form of a report (without subheadings) or a letter. Imagine you really want the child to win the award.

5   An international children's society offers annual awards to children who have shown examples of great bravery. Candidates for the award have to be nominated by a relative or friend who must submit a detailed account of the circumstances involved. Prepare an application, describing the child you wish to nominate, explaining exactly what happened, and saying why you think they deserve to win an award.

Write your **application**.

Part 1

For questions **1–15**, read the article below and then decide which word on page **86** best fits each space. Circle the letter you choose for each question. The exercise begins with an example (**0**).

Example: 0 B

Talking rubbish

Lasanda Kurukulasuriya takes a Sri Lankan view of recycling

Reduce! Re-use! Recycle! The message hits Canadian (**0**) ... through all the media. As newcomers from Sri Lanka, we compare the situation here with the one back home. We may not be the most environmentally (**1**) ... citizens in the world but, compared with this, we do not have a rubbish problem – yet.

Like many shoppers in Colombo, my partner Shahid and I used to have a cane basket we (**2**) ... with us to the market every week. No environmentalist could have (**3**) ... about it. There are no supermarket (**4**) ... to push around. Most items – rice, flour, vegetables, biscuits – are bought (**5**) ... or wrapped in newspaper. At (**6**) ... we would carry one plastic bag and a reusable plastic tray for eggs.

When income (**7**) ... are low, people need to buy in small quantities. It is quite normal to ask for a (**8**) ... envelope, two eggs or 100 grams of sugar. The (**9**) ... is that most shoppers in Sri Lanka cannot **afford** the luxury of waste. They re-use whatever they can and are loath to discard bags, jars or boxes that can be (**10**) ... to other uses.

But in recent years Western-style supermarkets have begun to spring up in Colombo. They hold out the (**11**) ... of a clean, efficient service to customers. A (**12**) ... of imported goods, dressed up in layers of attractive, colourful (**13**) ... beckons from the shelves. These are the (**14**) ... products that demand your attention on the TV advertisements. (**15**) ... with them, Sri Lanka, like so many other developing countries, may have imported a problem that once never existed.

From *The New Internationalist*

0	**A**	customers	**(B)**	consumers	**C**	clients	**D**	buyers
1	**A**	qualified	**B**	concerned	**C**	worried	**D**	experienced
2	**A**	took over	**B**	took away	**C**	took along	**D**	took up
3	**A**	complained	**B**	criticised	**C**	disapproved	**D**	accused
4	**A**	wheelbarrows	**B**	wagons	**C**	trolleys	**D**	carriages
5	**A**	free	**B**	in pieces	**C**	bit by bit	**D**	loose
6	**A**	maximum	**B**	most	**C**	highest	**D**	best
7	**A**	rates	**B**	amounts	**C**	sizes	**D**	levels
8	**A**	simple	**B**	singular	**C**	single	**D**	sole
9	**A**	point	**B**	case	**C**	example	**D**	question
10	**A**	made	**B**	set	**C**	given	**D**	put
11	**A**	promise	**B**	advantage	**C**	evidence	**D**	sight
12	**A**	set	**B**	range	**C**	store	**D**	band
13	**A**	packets	**B**	packs	**C**	packaging	**D**	padding
14	**A**	very	**B**	just	**C**	similar	**D**	likely
15	**A**	In addition	**B**	As well	**C**	Among	**D**	Along

▶ **Question 3**

Think about the grammar! Only one of these verbs takes *about* as a preposition.

▶ **Questions 12 and 13**

Remember you need **exactly** the right word for the context. After you've finished this test, use a dictionary to check how each of these words is used.

Part 2

For questions **16–30**, complete the following article by writing each missing word in the space provided. **Use only one word for each space**. The exercise begins with an example (**0**).

Example: `| 0 | has                          |`   `| ▢ 0 ▢ |`

New £20 note to prevent forgeries

THE CENTRAL BANK (**0**) .... had to introduce a new £20 note to prevent (**16**) .... unintended "privatisation" of the note printing business by forgers, the Governor of the Central Bank, Mr Maurice Doyle, said when he unveiled the note in Dublin yesterday. It is (**17**) .... introduced to combat the increasing banknote forgery which has come about in recent years (**18**) .... a result of developments (**19**) .... photocopying and printing, he said. (**20**) .... with access to a high quality colour photocopier and the correct paper (**21**) .... make a copy of the old £20 note that was good enough to be passed unnoticed (**22**) .... a crowded shop counter, he added. Although forgery problems in Ireland are not comparable to (**23**) .... of the major international currencies, such as the dollar, the Irish £20 note has some "close cousins", said Mr Doyle.

The new note, which comes (**24**) .... circulation on Monday, incorporates several features that will make (**25**) .... harder to forge. It has a watermark incorporating the number 20 (**26**) .... a silver security thread which shows when the note is held up to the light. It also incorporates a hidden image of the letters IR, which can only (**27**) .... seen when the note is tilted towards the light, and microprinting (**28**) .... the front and reverse. The note also contains features that (**29**) .... enable visually impaired people to recognise it, including a mark that can be felt (**30**) .... the fingertips.

▶ **Question 21**

Check the tense by looking at the whole sentence. Notice that this is an example of reported speech.

From *The Irish Times*

Part 3

In **most** lines of the following text there is **one** unnecessary word. It is either grammatically incorrect or does not fit in with the sense of the text. For each numbered line **31–46**, write the **unnecessary** word in the spaces next to the question number below. Some lines are correct. Indicate these lines with a tick (✓). The exercise begins with two examples (**0**).

Examples:

0	✓		0
0	lives		0

THANK GOD IT'S MONDAY

0	The received wisdom is that our lives are more stressful than
0	those lives of any other age, that a combination of increased
31	workloads, job insecurity, the rapid social change and
32	unrelenting technological progress has been left us frazzled
33	and overburdened. But now it comes the backlash. A growing
34	band of academics, and doctors and psychologists believe that
35	stress is not always bad. They argue about that stress arousal –
36	where the body produces a burst of adrenalin – is not only
37	good for us, but fundamental to all our survival. In America,
38	this trend has become known as 'Thank God It's Monday',
39	in which employees will look forward to the exhilaration
40	of starting up another demanding working week. Nobody
41	is denying that the pressures of everyday existence but the
42	new breed of specialists warn that the current methods of
43	dealing with them which are inadequate and often dangerous.
44	Instead of trying to manage the stress of response with drugs
45	or relaxation techniques, we should really be exploiting it
46	and turning it over to our advantage, they argue.

From *The Times*

▶ Question 32

Check that auxiliary verbs are used correctly. Should this be a passive?

▶ Questions 40 and 46

Look carefully at phrasal verbs. Is the particle really needed in these sentences?

▶ Question 43

Remember to check that relative pronouns are used correctly.

31	35	39	43 ....
32	36	40	44 ....
33	37	41	45 ....
34	38	42	46 ....

Part 4

For questions **47–61** read the two texts below. Use the words in the boxes to the right of the texts, listed **47–61**, to form a word that fits in the same numbered space in the text. The exercise begins with an example (**0**).

Example: | 0 | *extinction* | | 0 |

Surfing the Web for your Holiday

The holiday brochure may be heading for (**0**) ... , according to Tony Bennett, the (**47**) ... of Britain's second largest travel agency, who this week (**48**) ... a new booking system. He believes that in ten years' time, (**49**) ... will find out everything they need to know about trips by looking at computer screens. Among the benefits, Bennett says, will be the end to grabbing (**50**) ... of brochures and then spending hours trying to decide which holiday suits you best. And it will be (**51**) ... sounder, wasting less paper. "Our computers will make people working in shops better (**52**) ... to find the right holiday for customers," Bennett said. "Eventually brochures will become (**53**) ... ."

(0)	EXTINCT
(47)	CHAIR
(48)	VEIL
(49)	HOLIDAY
(50)	ARM
(51)	ECOLOGY
(52)	EQUIP
(53)	DATE

Software Review

Do you find geography revision boring? Well, you shouldn't any more with the CD Rom, *Test for Success – Geography*. The program includes (**54**) ... multiple-choice tests on five key subjects: (**55**) ... skills, places, physical geography, human geography and (**56**) ... issues. Each question is followed by four possible answers and many are (**57**) ... by a diagram. When I answered a question correctly, an (**58**) ... flashed up beneath it. These were concise but (**59**) ... and are an excellent feature of a title which neatly clears up (**60**) ... . There are three levels of difficulty, each with its own batch of questions. A very useful, if potentially (**61**) ... , part of *Test for Success* was the complete record it made of my results.

(54)	EXTEND
(55)	GEOGRAPHY
(56)	ENVIRONMENT
(57)	COMPANY
(58)	EXPLAIN
(59)	INFORM
(60)	CONFUSE
(61)	DEPRESS

From *The Times*

▶ **Question 48**

veil means 'to cover or hide'. Add a prefix for the opposite meaning. Then make sure the tense is correct.

▶ **Question 50**

This needs a suffix describing a quantity. Should the answer be singular or plural?

47	....	52	....	57	....
48	....	53	....	58	....
49	....	54	....	59	....
50	....	55	....	60	....
51	....	56	....	61	....

Part 5

For questions **62–74**, read the following informal note about a meeting and use the information to complete the numbered gaps in the formal letter. **Use no more than two words** for each gap. The words which you need **do not occur** in the informal note. The exercise begins with an example (**0**).

Example: | **0** | unable | | ⬜ ⁰ ⬜ |

INFORMAL NOTE

Dear Debbie

Just a note to let you know that I can't come to the AGM next Thurs. Sorry about this, but my mum's got a few problems at home and I need to go and help sort things out.

You did say that if I couldn't make the meeting, you wouldn't mind standing in for me and I trust this is still OK. It's basically just a question of taking notes and saying a few words about the conference we organised in the summer.

I'll let the Chair know what we've arranged and I'll also mention my feelings about a couple of the items on the agenda. As you know, I'm dead against the idea of bumping up the annual membership fee for next year – I think we'd just lose members. On the other hand, I've no objection to bringing in a rule to stop people smoking at meetings.

Many thanks for helping out in this way.

Yours

▶ Notice that the style is very formal and that you will need to use some special expressions connected with the topic of meetings/committees.

FORMAL LETTER

Dear Madam Chair,

I regret to inform you that I will be (**0**) .... to (**62**) .... the Annual General Meeting which is to (**63**) .... on Thursday 27th, owing to the fact that I have some urgent family (**64**) .... to deal with.

My colleague, Deborah Brandon, has kindly (**65**) .... to take my (**66**) .... at the meeting and to give a brief (**67**) .... on the summer conference.

I should like to take this opportunity to comment on two of the agenda items. Firstly, I do not (**68**) .... the proposal to (**69**) .... the membership fee for the coming year. It (**70**) .... me that such a move would certainly (**71**) .... a (**72**) .... in membership numbers. I am, however, fully (**73**) .... of the move to (**74**) .... a ban on smoking at meetings.

Yours sincerely,

Part 6

For questions **75–80**, read through the following text and then choose from the list **A–J** the best phrase given below it to fill each of the spaces. Write one letter (**A–J**) in each space provided. **Some of the suggested answers do not fit at all.** The exercise begins with an example (**0**).

Example: 0 J   0

Book reading a lost art at Harvard
From Charles Bremner, New York

Hardly a day goes by without a fresh demonstration of the ignorance of America's first video generation. Illiteracy is growing, and a new poll shows that a quarter of university students have no idea when Columbus reached America.

Some institutions, at least, have until now been presumed to be above the decay. It was imagined, for example, that they were still reading books at Harvard. But that illusion, too, has been shattered by Professor Sven Birkerts, who teaches Creative Writing to undergraduates there. "(**0**) ... ," he says in a powerful lament which has just been published by *Harvard Magazine*. Every year, he says, he conducts a survey among his students, and "(**75**) ... ."

The Harvard undergraduates studying under Professor Birkerts are, to put it no higher, reluctant readers. "The printed page taxes and wearies them. (**76**) ... .

I read through their first papers, so neatly word-processed, and my heart sinks," he writes, adding: "(**77**) ... ".

Professor Birkerts said yesterday that the trend away from reading seemed to have reached a critical stage. "(**78**) ... . It's merely that they are no longer receiving the world through the medium of print," he said. "They find it difficult to sit in front of a stationary page."

Professor Birkerts wonders how his students imagine they can learn to write without bothering to read. He says that they give all kinds of explanations for their failure to read. "Too busy." "(**79**) ... ." "I've always had a hard time with books that are supposed to be good for me." And then, proudly: "If I have time, I like to relax with Stephen King (the popular novelist)."

Professor Birkerts adds: " (**80**) ... Very likely it will once again be flat."

From The Times

Question 78

The clue is in the following sentence, which seems to be correcting a possible wrong impression.

Question 75

The clue is in *survey* – do you think the results of this survey are likely to have pleased or saddened the professor?

A   The writing is almost always flat, monotonous prose
B   Most students have video recorders
C   It's not lack of interest
D   Their handwriting is poor
E   Will the world be different if people stop reading?
F   the responses are heartbreaking
G   I wish I had the time
H   They find little pleasure there
I   He doesn't think it's a serious problem

J   Almost none of my students reads independently

Paper 4 – Listening

Part 1

You will hear some information about places to visit in the historic harbour area of the City of Bristol. For questions **1–10**, fill in the missing information.

You will hear the recording twice.

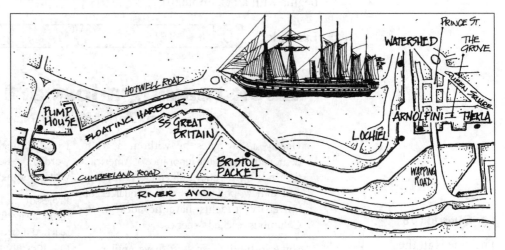

Name	Original Use	Current Use
Harbour	centre for commercial shipping	centre for leisure activities and **1**
Watershed	**2**	**3**
Arnolfini	**4**	**5**
Thekla	freight steamer	**6**
SS Great Britain	first ocean-going iron ship	**7**
Pump House	**8**	**9**
Bristol Packet	working narrowboat	**10**

▶ **Question 3**

Just give the key information – ignore any extra details.

▶ **Questions 8 and 9**

Be careful! The information isn't given in exactly the same order as the questions.

Part 2

You will hear the details of a recipe. As you listen, complete the information for questions **11–18**.

Listen very carefully as you will hear the recording ONCE only.

> ▶ **Questions 12 and 13**
>
> If you don't catch the information you need, listen carefully – the word you need may be repeated.

Tomato and Artichoke Salad with Basil

SERVES ☐ **11**

Ingredients

450g ☐ **12** tomatoes

400g can of artichoke hearts

1 small onion

1 large clove of garlic

half a lemon

3 tablespoons ☐ **13**

30ml fromage frais

salt and pepper and fresh basil

sprigs

Method

Drain artichoke hearts and ☐ **14**

Quarter the tomatoes. Place with artichoke hearts on

a suitable ☐ **15**

To make dressing

Roughly chop the onion.

Put crushed garlic, lemon juice, oil and fromage frais

and seasoning ☐ **16**

Mix well and add onion.

Pour over vegetables and basil.

Cover and chill for ☐ **17**

NOT SUITABLE ☐ **18**

Part 3

You will hear some advice about interviews. For questions **19–28** complete each of the statements.

You will hear the recording twice.

▶

Try to predict the answers to Questions 19, 22 and 28.

Your CV should be no longer than [_____ **19**]

It's important to think carefully about the content of your

[_____ **20**]

Make sure you stress any [_____ **21**] you've had.

Before the interview think about what you want to say,

and [_____ **22**]

If you don't know what you want to get across, the interview will be

[_____ **23**]

Including key information about yourself in your answers to questions

gives you more [_____ **24**] the interview.

▶ **Question 24**

Make sure you include a correct preposition in your answer (two are possible).

It's not a good idea to act like a [_____ **25**] salesperson.

It's no longer necessary to [_____ **26**] for an interview.

Appearance is particularly important in interviews for jobs which

involve [_____ **27**]

If you're not comfortably dressed, you're unlikely to

[_____ **28**] in the interview.

Part 4

You will hear five short extracts in which various people are talking about interview experiences. For questions **29–38**, choose the correct option **A, B** or **C**.

You will hear the recording twice.

▶

With multiple choice questions, remember to read through all the questions before you listen.

▶ **Question 29**

Be careful! The information you need comes at the beginning.

29 What was the first speaker's opinion of his interview?
    A It was quite frightening.
    B It was extremely difficult.
    C It wasn't very fair.

30 What does he think was wrong with his answer to a question?
    A He didn't tell the truth.
    B He didn't mention his qualifications.
    C He wasn't positive enough.

31 In the interview described by the second speaker,
    A he was tested on theoretical aspects of his work.
    B he was given a piece of equipment to repair.
    C he was asked about his experience and training.

32 When he was given a number of questions
    A he took a long time to answer them.
    B he answered most of them wrongly.
    C he didn't answer them at all.

33 The third speaker didn't feel at ease because
    A the atmosphere was very formal.
    B the seating was uncomfortable.
    C she wasn't dressed smartly enough.

34 Why does she think the interview went badly?
    A She hadn't prepared for the interview properly.
    B She didn't listen to the questions carefully.
    C She didn't give appropriate answers.

35 The fourth speaker particularly disliked
    A the questions she was asked.
    B the interviewer's manner.
    C the room where the interview took place.

36 What was the result of the interview?
    A She was offered the job and took it.
    B She was offered the job but didn't take it.
    C She wasn't offered the job.

37 The last speaker mentions an interview where
    A a number of applicants were interviewed together.
    B an applicant was interviewed by a group of people.
    C an applicant had several interviews with different people.

38 Why did things go wrong for the person being interviewed?
    A He was extremely anxious.
    B He became too relaxed.
    C He forgot what he was going to say.

Paper 5 – Speaking

Work with another student.

Part 1 (3 minutes) Introductions and General Social Conversation

Imagine you had never met your partner.

Remember to try to introduce some interesting points into the conversation.

- Introduce yourselves to each other.

- Tell your partner about your family. Ask them about theirs.

- Ask your partner what they enjoy watching on television. Explain what your favourite programmes are.

- Tell your partner what your ideal holiday would be. Ask your partner about their ideal holiday.

Part 2 (3 or 4 minutes)

In this part of the test you will each have the opportunity to talk for a minute.

Task 1

A Quiet Evening In (Describe and contrast)

You will each have the same set of pictures to look at.

Turn to the pictures on page 147.

Remember that in the exam the instructions will be **spoken** (not written down). It's important to listen very carefully so that you do everything required.

Candidate A: Talk to your partner about the people and activities shown, saying whether you think the pictures are a fair reflection of the ways different age groups prefer to spend their free time. You have about a minute for this.

Candidate B: Listen to your partner's description. When A has finished, say whether you agree with his/her comments. Which of these activities appeals to you most?

Task 2

City Views (Describe and identify)

Each candidate has four pictures of city scenes. Three of the pictures are the same but in a different order. One of the pictures is different in each case. Don't look at each other's pictures.

Don't worry if you can't think of the **exact** word for something. You won't lose marks if you find another way to express what you want to say.

Candidate B: Turn to the set of pictures on page 149 and describe them clearly so that your partner can identify them. You have about a minute for this.

Candidate A: Turn to the set of pictures on page 148. Listen to your partner's description and decide which picture is not described. When B has finished, describe the remaining picture.

Part 3 (3 or 4 minutes)

Cover Photo (Evaluate and rank-order)

In this part of the test you have to discuss a topic with your partner.

> Remember to keep the conversation going by using 'fillers' like *Now, let me see ...*, which give you time to think.

Your college or university is producing a new prospectus and you have been asked your opinion about which photograph to use on the front cover. Discuss the different aspects of college life which the photographs represent, and how much these would appeal to prospective students, then decide which you think are the best **three** in order of merit.

You have three or four minutes for this.

Part 4 (3 or 4 minutes)

In this part of the test you and your partner have to report on the outcome of your discussion in Part 3, saying whether you agreed or not. You then take part in a more general discussion with your partner and the examiner.

> You should both take part in this report-back stage. Be prepared to ask your partner if you've forgotten anything or to add any points your partner omits.

Practise your reporting and discussion skills by working with another pair. Take it in turns to summarise and explain the conclusions you reached, and discuss the following questions:

- If you were choosing a school or college to attend, what are the main things you would look for in the prospectus?

- When you're deciding on a course of study, is it important to choose one that will lead to a well-paid career? Why/why not?

- Is it better to live at home or to live in college while you're studying?

- What are the advantages and disadvantages of studying in another country?

- Are you influenced by the cover when you choose a book or magazine to read?

Practice Test 4
Paper 1 – Reading
Part 1

Answer questions **1–18** by referring to the review of children's educational books on page **99**.

> For questions **1–18** answer by choosing from the sections of the review (**A–H**). Some of the choices may be required more than once.
>
> Note: When more than one answer is required, these may be given **in any order**.

Which book or set of books

concerns history?	1	
contains useful lists of facts?	2	3 ....
has been published for many years?	4	
contains well-known sayings?	5	
has an introduction explaining how to use the book?	6	
includes maps?	7	8 ....
features lots of close-up photographs?	9	
features cartoon-style drawings?	10	
has sections which you can lift up or pull out?	11	

Which book or set of books does the author think

would be suitable for children under 10 years old?	12	
would also be suitable for adults?	13	14 ....
looks rather old-fashioned?	15	
is very good value for money?	16	
has pictures which are slightly ridiculous?	17	
is the best produced and most complete?	18	

How to find out about dinosaurs

A When buying an encyclopedia, you will find that the basic choice lies between fat single volumes, with useful but necessarily limited entries, and larger and costlier multi-volume sets. It is possible to purchase single volumes by subject area, which build up to form a comprehensive reference library, but none that I have seen compares for authority, design and breadth with the new **Oxford Children's Encyclopedia** (OUP £100). I cannot fault it. It is beautifully clear and has been laid out intelligently and attractively. Information is easy to find and children will gain confidence through learning how to cross-refer, and in the process will hit upon innumerable interesting side-shoots of information.

The encyclopedia uses a variety of illustrative styles: line drawings, cross-sections, maps, charts, diagrams and excellent photographs with good clear reproduction in sharp focus. Explanations are lucid, but there is some depth to them. Each entry gives basic information and has a See-Also box, to guide the reader further.

Every home with children would do well to buy a set and it is not to be despised by adults for their own use, either.

B The Dorling Kindersley **Children's Illustrated Encyclopedia** (£25) has the unmistakable design trademark of that firm – much use of large, close-up photographs of objects, clear typeface, good quality paper. It is divided into topics rather than arranged alphabetically. If you need to know about, say cork, you consult the index, and are referred to the section on trees, in which you will find your relevant paragraph. Once children have read the How to Use This Book pages at the beginning, they should have no problem in finding their way around. Whereas the Oxford set will suit children best as they progress towards their GCSE years, the Dorling Kindersley encyclopedia is a particularly good choice for the under-10s.

C That good old standby, **The Junior Pears Encyclopedia**, now in its 31st year and edited by Edward Blishen (Pelham £10.99), is a book to have handy by the homework desk for checking facts or giving brief explanations. It also contains those lists so beloved of a certain type of small boy: a Diary of World Events, The Highest Mountains in the World, Historic Acts of Parliament, Manned Spacecraft launched up to December 1990.

D Some of the non-fiction series now look dated and dreary, set against so much that is attractive and fresh. I wouldn't, for example, spend money on a series such as the **On the Map** (Simon and Schuster £4.99 each), one-volume introductions to countries of the world. Nothing new is attempted, with dull slabs of minimal text plonked beside uninterestingly arranged picture-library photographs of the usual French market, Eiffel Tower, Paris traffic variety. Altogether, it's a little too like a 1960s textbook to attract those buying books for home use.

E Geography is not easy to get right, but few inquisitive children could resist **The Picture Atlas of the World** (Dorling Kindersley £9.99). This is an absolute bargain, arranged alphabetically, with a two-page spread per country, beautiful maps, dotted with information in relief, and bordered by a section of Facts and Figures, a general paragraph of introduction, and some particularly important points highlighted in their own box. It brings the world alive.

F In a desperate effort to stave off children's boredom with historical topics, the **I Was There series** (Bodley Head £7.99 each volume) uses photographs of actors and extras dressed up and posing as Vikings battling, ancient Egyptians eating and writing on papyrus, medieval knights donning armour piece by piece. They look extremely unconvincing and rather silly.

G As a first thesaurus for children aged six and over, **The Kingfisher Book of Words** by George Beal (£7.99) is endlessly useful. Quotations, idioms and proverbs are cogently presented, well laid out and the whole book is cheered by cartoon-style line-drawings, illustrating for example, crocodile tears.

H Finally, I can recommend the perfect present for motor-mad infants – **Car** by Angela Royston and Colin King (Frances Lincoln £8.99). How a car works and how it can be mended are demonstrated and explained by flaps that can be lifted and tabs that can be pulled. Like all the best non-fiction for children, it is equally accessible to ignorant adults.

Part 2

For questions **19–24**, you must choose which of the paragraphs **A–G** on page **101** fit into the numbered gaps in the following newspaper article. There is one extra paragraph which does not fit in any of the gaps.

THERE'S PLENTY OF ROOM ABOARD PLANET EARTH

For decades the population explosion has been giving people nightmares. The world's human population increases by three every second and by a billion – equivalent to the present population of China – every decade. With figures such as these, the gloom has been understandable. In his 1968 book *The Population Bomb* Paul Ehrlich wrote: "The battle to feed all of humanity is over. In the 1970s the world will undergo famines; hundreds of millions of people are going to starve in spite of the crash programmes embarked upon now."

19

Today, environmentalists argue that the crisis has been deferred, not avoided. Like Malthus three centuries ago, they believe that the human race will ultimately outgrow its ability to feed itself. Were population to increase for ever, that would certainly be true. However, while the pundits have been worrying, people everywhere have been changing their habits.

World population is still rising fast, but it is already plain that the worst forecasts will never become reality. Far from reaching fifteen billion, nearly three times today's figure, the odds are that it may never get to ten billion.

20

In China, this is the result of tough government policies on family size, but, in many countries, including the United States and Brazil, it has been achieved without coercion. In most of Europe, the birthrate is now well below replacement level. In Italy, for instance, it is just 1.2 and it is not much higher in Spain or Germany.

So dramatic have been these changes that it is increasingly difficult to predict future population levels. One attempt, carried out by the International Institute for Applied Systems Analysis in Austria, attempted to include future changes in fertility along with such factors as mortality and migration. This exercise produced a wide range of projections of future population.

21

Some doubters question whether even the lower estimates will defer disaster. They claim the Green Revolution, which enabled food production to stay ahead of population growth, is faltering. The disaster which Paul Ehrlich so confidently and erroneously predicted for the 1970s could be waiting for us in the new millennium.

22

The new wheat, which is a product of the International Wheat and Maize Improvement Centre in Mexico, produces nearly double the yield compared with the other best varieties – a huge boost compared with recent progress.

23

In the past, economic growth has marched in step with population growth. So what will happen when populations decline? One effect is obvious: there will be fewer people of working age to support those in retirement, at least during the transition phase. Also, it may prove much harder to recruit people to do unpopular jobs.

24

Those who have painted a rosy picture of an environment recovering its natural beauty as the impact of human numbers declines could find that the opposite is nearer the truth.

From *The Times*

A Perhaps – but there seems no real reason for such pessimism. The improvements in plant productivity that made up the Green Revolution came from classical plant breeding, with no contribution from the new, and potentially far more significant, genetic technologies. And, as the recent launch of a new wheat variety in New Delhi makes clear, it is also not yet appropriate to write off classical methods.

B The change has come about because of dramatic drops in fertility in many countries. Replacement level, put at 2.1 children for each woman, has been reached in an increasing number of countries.

C Falling fertility and successes such as these show that there is at least a case for feeling optimistic about the future. Paradoxically, the greatest problems may come not from soaring populations but from the declines now beginning to become evident in some developed countries.

D He was wrong. Like other scientists, he underestimated the effects of the Green Revolution, which was transforming agricultural productivity even as he wrote. But he was at least in good company. The physicist Lord Blackett spent much of the 1960s worrying about how India was going to feed its millions, even as new varieties of wheat and rice were making that task easier.

E Dr Lutz believes the "ideal" figure achieved in the world in which both fertility and mortality are low would be a population of 6.5 billion by the year 2100. That seems pretty unlikely, even to optimists, but Dr Lutz gives it a 60% chance of coming true.

F Even maintaining the infrastructure of modern society could become harder as the tax base grows smaller. People hate to see the village school or the local hospital close, but that becomes inevitable when there are fewer children to teach or patients to treat.

G Although the most likely peak figure was predicted to be about 10 billion, much lower figures were not ruled out. According to Dr Wolfgang Lutz, who edited the institute's report, "The widespread pessimism about population explosions is exaggerated. What we have shown is that we can see the end of population growth on the horizon."

Part 3

Read the following newspaper article and then answer questions **25–30** on page **103**.
Indicate the letter **A, B, C** or **D** against the number of each question **25–30**.
Give only one answer to each question.

CURING THE ILL-MANNERED

Amateur actress Margaret Davies knows what it is to suffer for her art: over the past few years she has played characters with arthritis, severe depression, thyroid disturbances and mysterious dizzy spells.

Davies is a simulated patient, her roles based on real case histories but replayed as authentically as possible to medical students as part of their course in communication skills.

The project at Leicester University is in the vanguard of a campaign to put such skills at the centre of medicine rather than at its periphery. As senior lecturer Brian McAvoy explains, "Good communication is not just the icing on the cake. It's an essential part of being a competent physician."

Doctors' failings in this area are legendary. It is a rare patient who has never encountered at least one example of impatience, indifference, abruptness, tactlessness, insensitivity or just downright rudeness. All too often bedside manners are indistinguishable from bad manners.

Dr David Pendleton, editor of the book *Doctor–Patient Communication*, says the problem starts with the selection of students, when a certain kind of academic prowess is emphasized to the exclusion of other vital qualities. Training makes matters worse: "If something can't be medicalized it's not thought to be the doctor's province, so normal communication gets lost. We then overwork them so badly it's hard for them to retain what last scrap of humanity they might have."

Pendleton would like to see a selection process that taps into motivation, for example, without forfeiting academic excellence, plus more career guidance within the profession so that those who are neither interested in nor good with people could be directed towards the laboratory rather than the surgery.

Doctors are well aware of the communication problem. For his doctorate Pendleton carried out a study in the Oxford region and found that the doctors thought there was a barrier in about a quarter of their consultations. Key factors included the patient being a lot younger than the doctor, the patient being very tense, confused or shy and the patient being of a lower social class. The sex of either party did not seem to matter, nor did the length of the doctor's experience.

In McAvoy's sessions a student's tutor and peers can comment on his approach and the "patient" can step out of role and join the discussion.

Davies and her fellow actors are briefed in the character's personality as well as medical history. In this way students can encounter aggression, reticence and garrulousness. Sessions are replayed on video later. McAvoy believes the feedback from a simulated patient is invaluable. "Real patients may be afraid or embarrassed to say, for instance, that the spontaneous hand on the shoulder was very much appreciated or that they disliked the way the doctor wouldn't look them in the eye."

His course in the Department of General Practice is rare in being compulsory. Many schools make communication an optional extra if they offer it at all.

There is, however, growing awareness of its importance. The UK Network for Communication in Health Care was founded recently by interested professionals, to push for more and better teaching at every level.

Penny Morris is the network's convenor and a research and teaching fellow in communication skills at Cambridge University attached to Addenbrooke's Hospital. "Of course there are those who believe that though this sort of thing is important it can't actually be taught. But on the whole there is now an enormous amount of goodwill among doctors to learn.

People are not fooled by a smooth manner. They don't want to be reassured and fobbed off, they want information. Good communication is not just about being nice and charming, because you can have bags of charm and still be a disaster. Nor is it about teaching doctors manipulation skills. Simple things such as courtesy and patience are important because they are about valuing people. They imply a basic respect. And we like to stress that doctors who do these things have a better time, the difficulties are more bearable, the job more enjoyable."

From *The Times*

25 Margaret Davies is able to help with the project at Leicester University because
  A she trained as a medical student.
  B she has had personal experience of several illnesses.
  C she is a skilled teacher.
  D she can play the role of a patient realistically.

26 Examples of doctors' poor communication skills
  A are greatly exaggerated.
  B are widely known.
  C are the subject of many jokes.
  D are rarely encountered.

27 Dr Pendleton believes that the situation could be improved by
  A raising the academic standards of medical courses.
  B attracting more people to join the medical profession.
  C improving the process of selecting medical students.
  D making medical students work in laboratories more.

28 Research has shown that doctors find difficulty in communicating with patients when
  A the doctor is extremely tired.
  B the doctor is relatively inexperienced.
  C there is a big age gap between doctor and patient.
  D the patient is in pain.

29 Actors are particularly useful in training sessions because they
  A are able to discuss their reactions to a doctor's approach openly.
  B can replay the same consultations more than once.
  C are not embarrassed about discussing their medical symptoms.
  D can show stronger emotions than real patients.

30 According to Penny Morris, improved communication skills can lead to
  A more patients attending doctors' surgeries.
  B increased job satisfaction for doctors.
  C a higher success rate in treating disease.
  D greater respect for doctors from the public.

Part 4

Answer questions **31–49** by referring to the newspaper article about travel agencies on page **105**.

For questions **31–49** choose your answers from the list of travel agents (**A–E**) which are mentioned in the article. Some choices may be required more than once.

Note: When more than one answer is required, these may be given **in any order.**

In which travel agencies did the travel consultant

recommend a holiday in Portugal?	**31**	
suggest various places in Turkey?	**32**	**33** ....
praise the beaches in North Africa?	**34**	
provide detailed information about car hire services?	**35**	
suggest staying in an apartment rather than a hotel?	**36**	
have personal experience of a place they recommended?	**37**	**38** ....
check the possibility of flying from airports in cities other than London?	**39**	**40** ....
fail to mention that flights departed mid-week?	**41**	
pay no attention to the customer until he asked for help?	**42**	
recommend a place which was too noisy?	**43**	**44** ....
know about, or give full details of, the company's insurance policy?	**45**	**46** ....
advise the customer to use local public transport rather than rent a car?	**47**	
go in search of holiday information which was not on display?	**48**	**49** ....

Looking for the special agents

Most people turn to their high street travel agent when they decide to book a package holiday. But how do you know which ones will provide the personal service you want and suggest options to fit your criteria? EDWARD WELSH sought help at 12 branches, some of which came up with answers.

To test the leading travel agency chains, I visited a branch of each and sought help in selecting a package for four people: myself, my wife – we are both in our twenties – and her middle-aged parents. I outlined our requirements as follows:

- A two-week Mediterranean holiday in July, staying in a four-star hotel with half-board at a cost of up to £500 each. The accommodation should be by the sea but in a spot that was not too noisy or crowded and was close to interesting places to visit.

My other questions were:

- Could car hire be arranged?
- Could my wife's parents fly out from a different airport?
- Would it be possible to have full details of the agency's holiday insurance policy?

travel agent A

Margaret did not take long to work out what kind of holiday would suit my group. Ignoring all the brochures on show, she disappeared for a few minutes to find a selection of literature and began working out in which resorts we could afford to stay. This narrowed our choice to North Africa and Italy.

She felt Tunisia and Morocco would be excellent for beaches – and there would be some excursions to archeological remains and bazaars – but her real enthusiasm was for Italy. After tirelessly searching for somewhere within our price range we settled on Sorrento, a town she herself had visited. Her view was that there were excellent places to visit from Sorrento and, although the beaches were not fantastic, it was possible to swim in the sea.

The two hotels Margaret suggested were within our budget, but – and this she failed to point out – only as long as we didn't opt for a sea view.

Nonetheless, I was impressed by her knowledge and confidence and by the fact that she was conversant with her agency's travel insurance policy and could provide me with its details in full.

travel agent B

Although the agency was relatively busy, Nicole was happy to devote some time to helping me. Twice she went to a back office to dig up the brochures of smaller, more specialist tour operators whose literature was not displayed in the front office. And she was full of ideas for places to holiday.

But despite the hard work, she appeared to know little about the holidays she was trying to sell. Her suggested destinations included noisy, crowded Greek islands, such as Kos or Mykonos, or equally unsuitable parts of Turkey. She did not make me aware that flights to some of these Greek destinations only leave mid-week – an important detail for someone who can only take weekend to weekend holidays. From the brochures she was recommending, she was unable to find a four-star hotel that was within our budget, although at least one such does exist. She therefore began putting forward the idea of staying in apartments or villas, or going instead to Menorca or Ibiza.

Nicole knew nothing about the insurance policies on offer: she was either new to the job or lacked confidence in her own judgement. In terms of seeking useful information, I was wasting my time.

travel agent C

With only two counter staff and dozens of people pouring in every hour I was amazed that Lynn spent one hour and 10 minutes trying to help me find the right kind of holiday. But, despite her conscientious work, her advice only directed me to two of Turkey's more over-run resorts.

Working from the Go Turkey brochure, Lynn pointed out the fact that the prices listed did not include flight supplements and she suggested we forget car hire because public transport was so reliable and cheap – good advice. For any information she did not know, she contacted the tour operator. But most importantly, Lynn checked the availability of flights from Manchester and Gatwick and hotels I had selected. This was useful because one of my selections was fully booked at the time I was supposed to stay there.

In the end, we found that there was space at a suitable hotel near Bodrum in a relatively isolated spot near this still-attractive, yet busy town. The other option was a "B" class hotel close to the centre of Kusadasi, a noisy tourist-oriented town but with first-class access to the incredible classical sites in the region. Of the hotel, the brochure itself warns: "some noise is possible from a nearby bar/restaurant".

A pity, I thought, that Lynn had spent so long helping me with such uninspiring results.

travel agent D

Judith put a lot of effort into helping – tirelessly checking availability and prices – but few of her suggestions passed the "I'd be tempted" test.

Her first idea was Majorca which she had visited herself, but the two hotels she suggested – although in a sandy bay away from the island's largest resort – were modern high-rise blocks. Judith came up with many other recommendations such as the Costa del Sol, Cyprus and Crete, warning me off their noisier areas.

She handed me a useful leaflet listing car hire services throughout the Mediterranean and a copy of the agency's travel insurance which listed details in full.

Judith's hard work has to be commended but she was directing me towards the more expensive resorts or hotels in mass-market areas in the Mediterranean.

travel agent E

With the shop stuffed with travel consultants, you would have thought that a customer might receive some useful, personalised advice. But in fact this was supermarket holiday shopping of the highest order.

I was ignored until I asked for advice and, despite Liz's attachment to her computerised booking screen, she was unable to hide the glazed look of indifference on her face. She desultorily picked up Intasun's 260-page brochure and recommended the Algarve in Portugal.

She checked flight availability from Manchester and Birmingham and worked out the total costs per person including all the supplements. But, despite the computer wizardry, Liz was unable to find many affordable options. She suggested a three-star or four-star hotel in the centre of Faro away from the beach and – when I asked about other resorts – she came up with Malta and Lanzarote. She added that it was up to me to decide because there are "millions" of places to holiday and she did not really know what kind of package I was looking for. This came as no surprise at all.

Paper 2 – Writing

Part I

1 You are going to attend a one-month English language course in Britain and have asked for accommodation with a local family. You have just received two letters, one from the language school and one from the host family, and it is clear that the accommodation which has been arranged is not suitable.

You need to write to the school, pointing out the problems with the accommodation and asking for alternative arrangements to be made. In addition, you have to contact the family to explain that you will not be coming to stay.

Read the extracts from the letters and the handwritten notes you have made on them. Then, **using the information carefully**, write the two letters as instructed on page 107.

I am writing to tell you that I have arranged family accommodation for you from 2nd to 28th March, as requested. You will be staying with Mr and Mrs Hall at the address overleaf.

I said I'd be arriving on 1st.

The cost for this accommodation is £75 per week.

I said £70 max

Mrs Hall is writing to you separately and I would be grateful if you could contact her to confirm these arrangements and give details of your arrival time.

Yours sincerely,

Jane Woolworth

Jane Woolworth (Accommodation Officer)

I asked for somewhere quiet!

What a nerve!

Hardly local! much too inconvenient

out of the question – I stipulated a single room

We are delighted that you are coming to stay with us and we look forward to meeting you on 2nd March.

In the meantime, I thought we'd tell you something about ourselves. We have three lively children, Emma (4), Tom (7) and Harry (14) as well as four cats and a dog! We hope you like music – Tom has just started learning the violin, while Harry plays the electric guitar and his dearest wish is to play in a rock band!

We are hoping you'll be willing to do some baby-sitting for us while you're here, as my husband and I like to go out two or three nights a week.

Our house is about 10 minutes' walk from the village of Churchill. Buses go into town every two hours and the journey takes about 40 minutes. There is another bus from the city centre to the school.

The school said you wouldn't mind sharing a room with another student and we're now waiting to find out who your room-mate will be.

We hope to hear from you soon,

Brenda Hall

Brenda Hall (Mrs)

Now write:

a) a brief **letter** to Mrs Hall (approximately 50 words);
b) a **letter** to the school (approximately 200 words).

You should use your own words as far as possible.

Part 2

Choose **one** of the following writing tasks. Your answer should follow exactly the instructions given. Write approximately 250 words.

2 You have seen this announcement in an English language magazine and have decided to enter.

★ ★ ★ **Be a radio star!** ★ ★ ★

'English Alive', your local English language radio station, has been on the air for one year.
And now our airtime is to be doubled!
To celebrate, we are holding a competition
to find the best suggestions for new programmes
for the coming year.

The winner will appear as a guest presenter
on **'English Alive'**.

To enter, send clear details of the programmes
you suggest and explain why you think
they would be of interest to **'English Alive'** listeners.

Write your competition **entry**.

3 You have been asked by a college magazine to write an article aimed at new students, entitled *Studying Successfully: A Beginner's Guide*, which should be light-hearted but helpful. Describe the facilities available and mention a range of good study habits, recommending the ones which you have personally found most helpful.

Write the **article**.

4 This is part of a letter you receive from a friend.

> As you know, I'm planning to spend a year in your country before going to university. I've only been on short visits before but I'd really like to get to know the country better. The big question is: What should I do in the time? Attend a course? Be an au pair? Do voluntary work? I'd like to be near other students and I'd also need somewhere to stay that's not too expensive.
> I'd really appreciate any ideas or practical suggestions you could give me.

Write your **letter**.

5 An English friend is doing a project on 'green' issues round the world and has written to ask you about attitudes towards nature conservation and the recycling of waste materials in your country.

Write a **report**.

Paper 3 – English in Use

Part I

For questions **1–15,** read the article below and then decide which word on page **110** best fits each space. Circle the letter you choose for each question. The exercise begins with an example (**0**).

Example: | 0 | C | | 0 |

Hotels pick up bills for five-star thieves

For the latest (**0**) ... of *AA Hotels and Restaurants in Britain and Ireland* the AA (**1**) ... 2,000 hotels about the way their guests behave. The survey proves, the AA says, that the (**2**) ... the hotel's star rating, the greater its bill for thieving guests. Brian Sack, manager of a hotel on Ullswater, noticing a guest with three ashtrays in her handbag, deftly (**3**) ... two of them with the gentle reproof that one should be enough.

Thefts (**4**) ... from the petty: TV remote control batteries, light (**5**) ... , room numbers and fire assembly (**6**) ... , to the major: grandfather clocks, two beds, a stuffed bear and a complete (**7**) ... of onions taken from the garden of a hotel in Jersey.

Some hotels suffered quite serious (**8**) ... . One had its front door kicked down by three soldiers who had been (**9**) ... out. At the Seckford Hall Hotel in Suffolk, a sleepwalking guest wrenched a radiator off the wall, (**10**) ... rooms. One manager (**11**) ... "my nose" under items which had been broken.

Things guests (**12**) ... behind included false teeth, wigs, a sack of snakes and a box of poisonous spiders.

Hoteliers said that some guests' complaints were ridiculous. Bad weather (**13**) ... offence, though other natural phenomena that (**14**) ... guests included birdsong and the sound of the sea. One guest at the Seacrest Hotel in Hampshire, complained to the tourist board about a hurricane that had (**15**) ... him awake. The roof of the hotel had blown off.

From *The Times*

0	**A** copy	**B** example	**C** edition	**D** release
1	**A** examined	**B** checked	**C** questioned	**D** reviewed
2	**A** bigger	**B** higher	**C** more expensive	**D** more famous
3	**A** withdrew	**B** pulled	**C** stole	**D** removed
4	**A** range	**B** spread	**C** reach	**D** cover
5	**A** bulbs	**B** bells	**C** balls	**D** tubes
6	**A** signals	**B** notes	**C** notices	**D** advertisements
7	**A** bunch	**B** crop	**C** bundle	**D** flock
8	**A** damages	**B** breakages	**C** injury	**D** destruction
9	**A** closed	**B** stuck	**C** barred	**D** locked
10	**A** flooding	**B** overflowing	**C** spilling	**D** draining
11	**A** named	**B** explained	**C** marked	**D** listed
12	**A** let	**B** forget	**C** leave	**D** lose
13	**A** made	**B** caused	**C** produced	**D** did
14	**A** upset	**B** resented	**C** embarrassed	**D** hurt
15	**A** held	**B** brought	**C** made	**D** kept

Part 2

For questions **16–30**, complete the following article by writing each missing word in the space provided. **Use only one word for each space.** The exercise begins with an example (**0**).

Example: 0 an   0

THE IDEAL HOME THAT COLLAPSED IN MINUTES

Five months of expensive home renovation have finally come to (**0**) ... end for the Willis family. Their house fell down.

As builders worked (**16**) .... underpinning their £750,000 three-storey Victorian home in Notting Hill, West London, a small crack appeared. (**17**) .... minutes, the house began to disintegrate. (**18**) .... raising the alarm, six pale-faced builders (**19**) .... only stand and watch as the whole building came down. More than 50 people (**20**) .... evacuated from a nearby care centre for the disabled, and firefighters rescued a girl aged six (**21**) .... the house next door after rubble blocked the exits.

Stephen Willis, a mining company director, his wife Victoria and their three children had been living in rented accommodation (**22**) .... the work, which was (**23**) .... include repairs and a rear extension, was carried out. Mr Willis said: "This is devastating. We loved the area." His children reacted (**24**) .... the news "surprisingly well" but his wife was very upset, he said. The family hope to rebuild (**25**) .... the same spot, once they hear (**26**) .... insurance companies.

Peter Docherty, contracts manager for their builders, said he had no idea what (**27**) .... the property collapse. They had delegated the underpinning work (**28**) .... specialist subcontractors. He said: "We are sure it was a fault with (**29**) .... existing structure. It was (**30**) .... we couldn't have foreseen."

Part 3

In **most** lines of the following text there is either a spelling or a punctuation error. For each numbered line **31–46**, write the correctly spelled word(s) or show the correct punctuation in the space provided. Some lines are correct. Indicate these lines with a tick (✓). The exercise begins with three examples (**0**).

Examples:	**0**	✓		0
	0	television, video		0
	0	Government		0

TV ON–OFF SWITCH MAY HELP TO SAVE PLANET

0 A campaign to counter global warming by persuading households

0 to turn off the television video and computer rather than leaving

0 them on standby will be launched today. Goverment ministers

31 will highlight research showing that the simplest of actions if

32 followed by all households, would have a dramatic affect in

33 cutting carbon dioxide emissions. They will point to studies

34 showing that some electrical apliances use 80 per cent as much

35 energy on standby as when theyre fully working. A television set

36 left on for four hours a day, then put on standby will consume

37 roughly the same amount of energy as a fan heater running for

38 one hour. "The amounts of electricity for each gadjet may seem

39 quite small. But because there are 60 million of us in these

40 islands, it adds up to quite a lot, said Michael Meacher, the

41 Enviroment Minister. He and other ministers believe that

42 winning householders over to a more efficient use of energy

43 is a key to meeting international targetts for cutting greenhouse

44 gases. In addition to the problem in the home the service

45 sector and industry will also be targeted. Retaling, banking and

46 insurance create more gases than the iron, steal and chemical

industries combined.

---

31 .... 35 .... 39 .... 43 ....

32 .... 36 .... 40 .... 44 ....

33 .... 37 .... 41 .... 45 ....

34 .... 38 .... 42 .... 46 ....

Part 4

For questions **47–61** read the two texts below. Use the words in the boxes to the right of the texts, listed **47–61**, to form a word that fits in the same numbered space in the text. The exercise begins with an example (**0**).

Example: | **0** | *Medical* | | **0** |

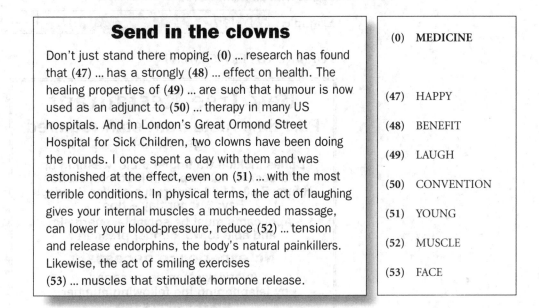

Send in the clowns

Don't just stand there moping. (**0**) ... research has found that (**47**) ... has a strongly (**48**) ... effect on health. The healing properties of (**49**) ... are such that humour is now used as an adjunct to (**50**) ... therapy in many US hospitals. And in London's Great Ormond Street Hospital for Sick Children, two clowns have been doing the rounds. I once spent a day with them and was astonished at the effect, even on (**51**) ... with the most terrible conditions. In physical terms, the act of laughing gives your internal muscles a much-needed massage, can lower your blood-pressure, reduce (**52**) ... tension and release endorphins, the body's natural painkillers. Likewise, the act of smiling exercises (**53**) ... muscles that stimulate hormone release.

(**0**)	MEDICINE
(**47**)	HAPPY
(**48**)	BENEFIT
(**49**)	LAUGH
(**50**)	CONVENTION
(**51**)	YOUNG
(**52**)	MUSCLE
(**53**)	FACE

YOUR MOOD MAY BE CATCHING

Moods are contagious – and that's official. Scientists have proved that you can catch joy or (**54**) ... like colds or flu, whether you want to or not, (**55**) ... at work. Though scientists have been interested in crowd (**56**) ... and mass hysteria for more than a century, they have only recently started noticing that (**57**) ... is also (**58**) ... . John Addison, a department store assistant, was finding his work tedious and (**59**) ... . "The manager drained all the energy out of you," he says. "He was dour and (**60**) ... , and it was an effort to work at all when he was around. Then we got someone else who is funny, (**61**) ... , and who gives out a lot of energy, and I suddenly felt much warmer towards the job."

(**54**)	SAD
(**55**)	SPECIAL
(**56**)	BEHAVE
(**57**)	CHEERFUL
(**58**)	CATCH
(**59**)	REWARD
(**60**)	SUSPECT
(**61**)	LIVE

47 ....   52 ....   57 ....

48 ....   53 ....   58 ....

49 ....   54 ....   59 ....

50 ....   55 ....   60 ....

51 ....   56 ....   61 ....

Part 5

For questions **62–74,** read the following formal advertisement from the Positions Vacant column of a newspaper and use the information to complete the numbered gaps in the informal letter to a friend. **Use no more than two words** for each gap. The words which you need **do not occur** in the formal advertisement. The exercise begins with an example (**0**).

Example: | 0 | job |

FORMAL ADVERTISEMENT

Bay Tree Restaurant
Part-time restaurant staff required
Age: 16–24

Duties include waiting at table, washing up
and occasional help with food preparation
Hours: 7.30–11.30, Saturdays and/or Sundays
Pay: £10 per day + tips

Applicants must be sociable, energetic
and able to work under pressure.

No experience necessary

Interviews can be arranged
by telephoning the following number:
Bloxham 376152

INFORMAL LETTER

Dear Jenny,

You said you were looking for a part-time (0) .... and I thought you might be interested in an ad. I saw in the local paper. It's basically working as (62) .... in that new restaurant, The Bay Tree. But apart from (63) .... customers' orders and serving food, you also have to wash the (64) .... and even lend (65) .... with the cooking once in (66) .... – sounds fun! I know you've got a few hours to spare at (67) .... and there are two (68) .... shifts to choose from. They're looking for someone who enjoys (69) .... people and who can keep a (70) .... head when things get hectic, so you'd be ideal! You're also in the (71) .... age bracket and you don't even need to have done that kind of work (72) .... The basic pay's not great but the good thing is that (73) .... you get are yours to keep. If you're interested, why not give them (74) .... ? They'll be in the local directory.

Good luck!

Part 6

For questions **75–80,** read through the following text and then choose from the list **A–J** the best phrase given below it to fill each of the spaces. Write one letter (**A–J**) in each space provided. **Some of the suggested answers do not fit at all.** The exercise begins with an example (**0**).

Example: | 0 | J | | | 0 |

Health Advice for Travellers

Doctors tend to be poor educators; we have depressingly little to show for our efforts to educate the general public on even such a clear-cut issue as the effects of cigarette smoking on health. (0) ... is it for doctors to provide large numbers of departing travellers with detailed information and effective advice for their trip when the usual forum for doing so is a single, hurried consultation, just before departure. There are limits to what can be achieved in or should be expected from a medical consultation (75) ... , even when the doctor is well-informed about the subject, and the traveller is receptive, has a perfect memory, and is good at doing what he or she is told.

What kind of advice should travellers receive? A list of rules and instructions (76) ... carries the implication that travellers are incapable of understanding the principles involved, are not interested, or do not 'need' to know. (77) ... advice offered on such condescending terms is seldom followed for long. The best advice is not a list of dos and don'ts, but a clear, rational explanation from which a conclusion is obvious.

(78) ... , we have studiously avoided giving advice to consult a doctor without stating the reason for doing so. 'Consult your doctor' is a useful formula to enable advice-givers to avoid difficult issues, but is a particularly unhelpful one when it relates to a problem which may arise abroad. (79) ... to find a doctor in a remote place. Some 85% of the world's population have never seen a doctor, and never will. Advice for travellers must take account of the fact that travellers to many parts of the world will be (80) ... .

From Traveller's Health

A   It is hardly surprising that
B   But despite this
C   Throughout this book
D   It is essential
E   in the same position
F   given without explanation or justifications
G   It is not easy
H   based on the principle
I   under the best of circumstances

J   How much more difficult, then

Paper 4 – Listening

Part 1

You will hear some advice about preventing car crime. For questions **1–10**, fill in the missing information.

You will hear the recording twice.

Keep Your Car Secure

Having your car stolen leads to delay and [_____ **1**]

Remember that car crime is the most [_____ **2**] of all crimes.

Don't leave luggage and valuables [_____ **3**]

Never leave [_____ **4**] in the glove compartment.

Always lock the doors when you leave your car.

Have [_____ **5**] number etched on windows and other glassware.

Take the ignition key out even when your car is [_____ **6**]

Retract your aerial when you park.

Choose a security-coded radio/cassette machine or one which can be [_____ **7**]

Fit lockable wheel nuts to protect wheels.

A lockable fuel cap forces thieves to [_____ **8**] your car when it runs out of petrol.

Don't leave vehicle documents in the car – they could help a thief to [_____ **9**]

Park your car in a busy [_____ **10**] area.

Part 2

You will hear about a number of auction sales on a telephone information service. As you listen, complete the information for questions **11–19.**

Listen very carefully as you will hear the recording ONCE only.

LLOYDS FINE ART AUCTIONEERS
Opening Hours

Monday to Friday: 9.00 a.m.–5.30 p.m.

Sunday: ⬚ **11** (for special viewing)

March

2nd   Old Master Paintings

3rd   ⬚ **12**

4th   Books, Atlases and Maps

8th   ⬚ **13**

(Estimated prices: £100– ⬚ **14**)

10th   Rock and Pop Memorabilia

16th   ⬚ **15**

19th   Classic Cars (held at Filton ⬚ **16**)

25th   Toys – including several antique ⬚ **17**

Sales on view for ⬚ **18** before auction.

Phone 071 543 2021 to order ⬚ **19**

Part 3

You will hear part of an interview with a doctor on the subject of jet lag. For questions **20–29** complete each of the statements.

You will hear the recording twice.

Jet lag is defined as a slight sense of _____ and _____ |20| after a long journey by air.

The doctor explains that our body rhythms are affected by clock time, _____ |21| and whether it's day or night.

The symptoms of jet lag include problems with _____ |22| and eating.

More importantly, jet lag can affect one's mental and physical _____ |23|

Recovering from jet lag takes about one day for each _____ |24| you've crossed.

Your recovery rate can be affected by the climate and even _____ |25| of the country you're going to.

You can buy anti-jet lag products but there's _____ |26| that they are effective.

To avoid jet lag, the doctor suggests trying to _____ |27| on the aeroplane.

He also advises against _____ |28|

He recommends that after arrival you avoid important commitments for _____ |29|

Part 4

You will hear five short extracts in which various people are talking about jet lag. For questions **30–39**, choose the correct option **A**, **B** or **C**.

You will hear the recording twice.

30 The first speaker believes that the degree of jet lag you suffer depends on
  A how frequently you travel.
  B the direction you travel in.
  C the length of the journey.

31 What is her advice?
  A Make sure you're well-rested before you travel.
  B Try to get as much sleep as possible on the plane.
  C Avoid being too energetic after you arrive.

32 The second speaker recommends that after arrival you
  A try to stay awake for 24 hours.
  B allow yourself to have a short sleep.
  C don't go to sleep until night-time.

33 He says that he
  A has always followed this system successfully.
  B doesn't always manage to follow this system.
  C usually fails to follow this system.

34 On arrival, the third speaker
  A doesn't try to adjust to the local time zone.
  B doesn't go to sleep until the sun sets.
  C doesn't drive in case he has an accident.

35 He also recommends
  A eating several meals.
  B eating a lot of sweets.
  C having lots of soft drinks.

36 When flying, the fourth speaker sometimes
  A stays awake worrying about his career.
  B finds it difficult to get to sleep.
  C can't help feeling very sleepy.

37 What does he feel it's necessary to do on arrival?
  A To go to bed as soon as possible.
  B To try to adjust to the local time.
  C To get down to work immediately.

38 The fifth speaker says she
  A has tried some strange treatments for jet lag.
  B follows her doctor's advice to avoid jet lag.
  C has found a way of eliminating jet lag.

39 One thing she does is to
  A take some exercise during the flight.
  B have a brief rest when she arrives.
  C go for a swim when she arrives.

Paper 5 – Speaking

Work in groups of three. One student should play the role of the examiner, giving instructions, asking further questions and making sure both candidates play an equal part in the conversation.

Part 1 (3 minutes) Introductions and General Social Conversation

Imagine you had never met your partner.

- The examiner and candidates introduce themselves.

- Tell the examiner a little bit about your partner.

- Ask your partner about a book you've really enjoyed reading. Ask your partner to tell you about the kind of reading he/she enjoys.

- Tell your partner about a sport you play or like to watch. Find out what sports your partner enjoys, if any.

Part 2 (3 or 4 minutes)

In this part of the test you will each have the opportunity to talk for a minute.

Task 1

Karate (Describe and identify)

You will each have a set of pictures showing karate moves. Don't look at each other's pictures.

Candidate A: Turn to the set of pictures on page 149 and describe them clearly so that your partner can identify them. You have about one minute for this.

Candidate B: Turn to the set of pictures on page 150. Listen carefully to your partner's description and decide which picture is not described. You may make notes if you wish. When A has finished, describe the remaining picture.

Task 2

Sale Time (Describe and comment)

You will each have the same pair of pictures, both taken by the same photographer, to look at.

Turn to the pictures on page 151.

Candidate B: Talk about the people in the pictures, saying what they're doing and how they might be feeling. What do you think the photographer was trying to show? You have about one minute for this.

Candidate A: Listen to your partner's description. When B has finished, say whether you agree with his/her comments. What kind of shopping do you enjoy least?

Part 3 (3 or 4 minutes)

Visit Britain (Evaluate and select)

In this part of the test you have to discuss a topic with your partner.

A tourist agency is planning an advertising campaign to encourage people to visit Britain. You have been asked for your views about the attractions which should be featured in the campaign. Decide which **three** should be included. Consider not only the ones which appeal to you and your partner but also those which might appeal to tourists of different ages and from different countries. You may, if you prefer, include a completely different attraction which you think is more suitable.

You have three or four minutes for this.

Part 4 (3 or 4 minutes)

In this part of the test you and your partner have to report on the outcome of your discussion in Part 3, saying whether you agreed or not. You then take part in a more general discussion with your partner and the examiner.

Practise your reporting and discussion skills by working with another pair. Take it in turns to summarise and explain the conclusions you reached, and then discuss the following questions:

- How much do you learn about a country if you only visit the capital city?

- What's the best way to meet the people in a country you're visiting?

- What research can you do to make a foreign holiday more enjoyable?

- Can you have a good holiday even on a tight budget? Why/why not?

- Is it better to travel alone or with one or two friends? Why?

- What are the advantages and disadvantages of taking a guided tour of a city?

Practice Test 5

Paper 1 – Reading

Part 1

Answer questions **1–18** by referring to the newspaper article about how travel writers take notes on page **123**.

For questions **1–18** answer by choosing from the list (**A–F**) on the right below. Some of the choices may be required more than once.

Note: When more than once answer is required, these may be given **in any order**.

Which travel writer or writers

found very low temperatures a problem?	**1**	
doesn't always understand the notes they've taken?	**2**	
made copies of their notes for safety?	**3**	**4** ....
was able to salvage their notes after an accident?	**5**	
has worked on a book with another author?	**6**	**7** ....
was very particular about the kind of notebook they used?	**8**	
has had books entered in a competition?	**9**	**10** ....
writes less during their travels than they used to?	**11**	
thinks notes have a limited value?	**12**	
temporarily lost their notes?	**13**	
always labels their notebooks carefully?	**14**	**15** ....
became ill during their travels?	**16**	
tries to take extremely detailed notes?	**17**	**18** ....

A Bruce Chatwin

B William Dalrymple

C Dea Birkett

D Eric Newby

E Sarah Wheeler

F Bill Bryson

NB: GET THAT SMELL DOWN ON PAPER

The passport can be replaced, but guard your notebook with your life. Mike Gerrard explores the world of the dedicated travel writer.

The late **Bruce Chatwin** only used notebooks with special bindings, bought in Paris. **William Dalrymple**, on the other hand, obtains his from any ordinary high street stationer's. It doesn't seem to have done him any harm, as he won the Thomas Cook/Daily Telegraph Travel Book Award for *City of Djinns* and is shortlisted again this year for *From the Holy Mountain*.

Whether precious, like Chatwin, or practical like Dalrymple, all travel writers have their idiosyncrasies. **Dea Birkett**, also shortlisted for this year's Travel Book Award for *A Serpent in Paradise*, always buys her notebooks when she is travelling, insisting on hardbacks to enable her to write while standing up. "Every notebook is different, but every one is special. It's my only travelling companion."

Birkett also buys her pens abroad. **Eric Newby**, however, prefers the humble pencil, and for good reason. During the journey that produced *A Short Walk in the Hindu Kush*, his horse went into a river, ruining his camera film. It would have destroyed his notebooks, too, had they been written in ink, but by chance, he had been using pencil.

Even worse conditions faced **Sarah Wheeler**, who spent several months in Antarctica researching *Terra Incognita*. "Everything froze – the ink in the pen and the lead in the pencil. I had to stow things about me to keep them warm."

Wheeler and **Birkett**, who together edited *Amazonians*, a collection of travel writing by women, both admit to obsessions. **Birkett** writes her name and the date and place of purchase inside the front cover of every notepad she buys, while **Wheeler** puts the destination on the spines of all of hers. "When the writing fades, I relabel them. I like to see them in a row on the shelf in my office with all the names standing out nicely."

So what goes into these carefully chosen and meticulously labelled pads? When **Bill Bryson** wrote *The Lost Continent*, his first travel book, it was almost everything. "It got to the stage where I found myself writing, 'spent time sitting in a café writing down notes'," Bryson recalls. "Sometimes something will strike me as interesting or amusing and I write down 'Don't forget big man in red braces', but when I come to write the book I have no recollection whatsoever of why I wrote it. I take more photographs now. Not great ones, but good enough to remind me of what a place like Nebraska looks like."

The casual approach might work for Bryson, but it won't do for **Birkett**. "If I don't write everything down, from the colour of the taxis to what the man standing next to me at the bus-stop said, then I'll miss something. When I get back home and trawl through my notes these things suddenly become crucial to the story, but while I was there I had no idea they would be."

Dalrymple agrees, "The key is to get everything down. What everyone says, the colours, the smells, they're the things which go if you don't do it immediately. I take illiterate on-the-minute notes – lists of details, sights, smells, sounds, very rarely written in good English – which I later transform into prose. The notebooks are the raw material."

Wheeler, by contrast, questions the value of meticulous notetaking. "I'm a slave to my notebook, but I'm also aware that I'll only become a great travel writer when I throw it away and write what I saw and felt from memory and imagination. I had altitude sickness at the South Pole and was too ill to take notes. I wrote a whole chapter from memory. It turned out no worse than any other."

Normally, however, for the writer returning home to produce a book for publisher and public, protecting the raw material is vital. "To lose a passport was the least of one's worries: to lose a notebook was a catastrophe," wrote **Chatwin**, who would post home carbon copies of his notes to avoid disaster.

Wheeler regularly relies on the security of the Diplomatic Bag, while **Dalrymple**, halfway through his journey around the Middle East, photocopied his notepads and posted them back to England.

Near-catastrophes come with the territory. When **Eric Newby** was going *Slowly Down the Ganges*, he left his notebook behind at a railway station. He only realised when he woke up at two o'clock in the morning, miles away from the station. "I got a cycle-rickshaw all the way back to the station. Thankfully I found it on a trolley where an Indian ticket clerk had put it. I went in to thank him, but he just said, 'Oh sir, it is a matter of no consequence. It's only a work of literature and of no interest to anyone.'"

Part 2

For questions **19–24**, you must choose which of the paragraphs **A–G** on page **125** fit into the numbered gaps in the following newspaper article. There is one extra paragraph which does not fit in any of the gaps.

Guru to New York's pampered pooches

Georgie the labrador spends much of the day on the balcony of a penthouse in Manhattan with views across the Hudson River. But his excitement erupts when Martin MacKinnon arrives because it means it's time for a walk.

19

Georgie's owner struck up an immediate rapport with Mr MacKinnon. So much faith did she have in him, in fact, that she had no qualms about giving him a key to her apartment as well as entrusting her precious Georgie to his care. "He loves all the dogs, which is the reason we let Georgie go with him," says the owner.

20

"He plays with them as if he were a dog himself and they get a level of exercise unheard of in New York," adds Georgie's owner. "He runs for hours with the dogs while other walkers might give them 30 minutes at most. He gives them so much attention that the dogs are crazy about him."

21

Among these he can number a leading socialite who owns a retriever, and Diann Duthie, a film-set designer with a labrador. Such people demand the best and Ms Duthie labels Mr MacKinnon as New York's dog-walking guru. "He gives dogs a quality of life that no other walker can offer," she says. Many owners take their puppies to expensive behaviour classes, but they still expect Mr MacKinnon to contribute to obedience training and stimulation.

22

Once in the park, he heads for secret stores of tennis balls he keeps in trees. This booty is down to a retriever, which finds them near the park's tennis courts. The dogs are even allowed a swim in the lake. Mr MacKinnon concentrates on "fun dogs" and fights shy of neurotic owners who would get upset if their dog returned wet and dirty.

23

That experience apart, Mr MacKinnon enjoys considerable job satisfaction. "Just occasionally, I'm not in the mood but it's great to think that I make a living playing with dogs," he says. "I like my clients as people and would be happy to socialise with them. It's that bond which makes it easier walking their dogs," he says.

24

On an average day, Mr MacKinnon walks about 20 dogs, in several shifts, covering up to 25 miles a day no matter what the weather. "I can get exhausted but I'm fine as long as I keep going," he says. "My batteries fail as soon as I sit down." His weekly income can reach $1,000 with a charge of $15 per dog per walk. "I'm making good money and having fun being outside," he says. "I say 'God bless America'."

A This selectiveness in the clients he is willing to accept clearly pays off. On only one occasion has he had to refuse to exercise a dog again – after it ran out of Central Park and across busy streets. "That was scary and I wouldn't have the confidence to let it go a second time," he explains.

B Like many New Yorkers, Georgie's owner walks him before leaving for the office. Mr MacKinnon takes care of day-time exercise by walking him every day for an hour in Central Park. "Because we're so busy, Georgie only gets real exercise when Martin takes him out," says the dog's owner. "We live in the city but Georgie gets more exercise than most country dogs." The exceptional service that Mr MacKinnon offers is clearly appreciated by his other regular clients too.

C Mr MacKinnon, a former forester on the Isle of Skye in Scotland, has established himself as New York's leading dog-walker, with many clients living in multi-million dollar apartments near Central Park, and there are now 45 dogs on his books.

D Daryl Hannah, the actress, left a telephone message asking him to walk her dogs while she was in New York, after a recommendation from Robert de Niro's dog-walker. Sadly, Mr MacKinnon was away and the actress had left by the time he got back. "But I still have the message to prove she called," he says.

E Indeed, that aspect of his job has had a particular significance for him. The relationship he established with his second client, Felicia Telsey, grew into romance over time and now they are happily married.

F However, like other security-conscious New Yorkers, she requests anonymity. Mr MacKinnon writes codes and colours on the apartment keys he's given, but never addresses or names. Such diligence cements his status, as does his affinity with animals.

G Mr MacKinnon already has some of his other dogs, including a rottweiler and another labrador, with him when he meets Georgie. When they leave the apartment block, eyes turn towards him as his gang pulls him towards Central Park. Exercise levels are geared to each dog, with older ones given shorter runs. However, a three-legged mongrel called Tricycle still remains one of the fastest.

Part 3

Read the following newspaper article and then answer questions **25–31** on page **127**. Indicate the letter **A, B, C** or **D** against the number of each question **25–31**. Give only one answer to each question.

No driving instructor would tell a learner: jump in, drive away and I'll tell you later how you've done. Yet every year trainee teachers are propelled into classrooms with only the promise of an assessment *after* the lesson they are giving, rather than guidance before or during it.

Dr Peter Tomlinson, a psychologist in Leeds University's school of education, believes the idea of the post-lesson debriefing is flawed. His new method, which bears a closer resemblance to that of the driving instructor, is radio-controlled teacher training: a system of monitoring using microphones, earpieces and transmitters which he calls RAP – radio-assisted practice.

To RAP, tutor and student each wear an earpiece, a four-inch two-way radio which can be hidden under a jacket, and a tiny microphone. The student wears the microphone on his or her clothes, so the tutor can hear what both student and nearby children are saying. The tutor straps his microphone on to a finger, so that he can unobtrusively speak into it directions, reminders, hints, criticisms and encouragement – all heard only through the student's earpiece.

It sounds complicated and distracting. Dr Tomlinson agrees, and most tutors who have tried it find they have to think harder about what they should be advising students to do, because they must be concise and clear. All but a handful of students quickly adjust to the tutor's interventions, on average every two to four minutes.

Sue Brown (not her real name) is in her second teaching practice of a Postgraduate Certificate of Education. She explained Dr Tomlinson's presence and wiring to her class of inner-city

High-tech practice as the tutor preaches

Novice teachers can now get on-the-job coaching via an invisible earpiece. **Karen Gold** *investigates*

10-year-olds by saying he was studying how teachers teach. It was her sixth day in school: long enough for her to discover that her charges were accustomed to control by criticism and shouting. Her aim for herself as a teacher was to resort to neither.

For art-and-craft she had brought in magazines, food packets and dried pulses for the children to make pictures on the theme of food. Before the lesson, she and Dr Tomlinson discussed how she would introduce the activity and agreed on their focus for RAPping: her positioning in the classroom, vital when children are spread around tables rather than lined behind desks: "scanning", or actively looking everywhere to see what children are doing; keeping the initiative, and not just reacting to attention-seeking or disruption.

At 11 am the children start on their pictures. Within minutes, half a dozen are wandering around. "If you want them at the tables, get them there and reiterate the rules," Dr Tomlinson says. Sue does. They settle. She moves around the classroom, squeezing between tables, stopping frequently. "Positioning," warns her tutor. She shifts to the wall side of the table, so she can see every child.

At 11.25, after a few interruptions, all is reasonably quiet. Even two notorious problem boys are absorbed. "Catch them being good," Dr Tomlinson says. Sue moves towards their table to reward their good behaviour with praise.

Before she gets there, a fight breaks out between two girls at another table. Sue defuses it but the calm is broken. Children start wandering around or squabbling. "Get them back on task," Dr Tomlinson says. "Will you all just sit down," Sue shouts, breaking a resolution. Then she hesitates. "Keep going," the voice urges in her earpiece. "Next time you won't be able to do this," she threatens. The children sit down sullenly. "Next time, nip it in the bud a bit earlier and tell them what *to do*, not what *not* to," Dr Tomlinson advises.

Sue, who is cutting more paper and trying to interest a boy who has done nothing so far, moves to stop the kicking and misses the dried-pea battle under way nearby. A boy ignores her order to move to another table. "Make sure he does it," Dr Tomlinson says. Sue does. "What should they be doing?" he prompts. Sue, sounding desperate, continues: "Will everybody just listen ... Calm down ..."

The lesson continues chaotically until the end when, at Dr Tomlinson's suggestion, Sue manages to get the children sitting down and dismisses them table by table.

From *The Independent on Sunday*

25 The new system of radio-assisted practice (RAP) is designed to
   A speed up teacher training.
   B make teacher training more effective.
   C cut the cost of teaching practice.
   D make teaching practice less frightening.

26 What problem have tutors found with the system?
   A They aren't used to giving advice briefly.
   B They have to speak quite loudly.
   C They can't hear what the children are saying.
   D They find it hard to think of any advice to give.

27 What was Sue Brown's aim for the lesson?
   A To control the children without raising her voice.
   B To be concise and clear in her instructions.
   C To avoid being criticised by her tutor.
   D To keep the pupils entertained during the lesson.

28 It was agreed that one focus of the RAP communication was to be
   A positioning the pupils round tables.
   B dealing with bad behaviour.
   C getting the pupils' attention.
   D being aware of everyone in the class.

29 During the first part of the lesson, Sue follows her tutor's advice by
   A moving the tables.
   B finding a different place to stand.
   C going to answer pupils' questions.
   D continuing to move round the classroom.

30 When the class is quiet, Sue's tutor suggests she goes to two boys to
   A check that they are really working.
   B give them prizes for behaving so well.
   C tell them how well they're working.
   D move them to different tables.

31 What is Sue too busy to notice later on?
   A a pupil who needs help
   B a boy who doesn't obey her
   C children starting to fight
   D children doing nothing

Part 4

Answer questions **32–46** by referring to the newspaper article about service around the world on page **129**.

For questions **32–46**, choose your answers from the list of cities (**A–F**). Some choices may be required more than once.

Note: When more than one answer is required, these may be given **in any order**.

In which city or cities		
are you likely to receive good service in a petrol station?	32	
can you have a telephone installed most promptly?	33	
did a researcher find long queues in a supermarket?	34	**A** Birmingham
can you have a washing machine delivered exactly when you want?	35	
did a researcher find a long queue in a bank?	36	**B** Glasgow
was there a problem with a bank's computer?	37	
are supermarket staff trained to respond politely to customers?	38	**C** London
was there a special offer on the price of a washing machine?	39	
might a bank pay **you**?	40	**D** Los Angeles
did a restaurant waitress accept a changed order with good humour?	41	
are banking services least efficient?	42	**E** Rome
could you wait the longest time for a washing machine to be delivered?	43	
did supermarket cashiers fail to react to the researchers' request?	44 .... 45	**F** Tokyo
could you wait the longest time for a telephone to be installed?	46	

You want your new washing machine delivered on Monday. Will you get it? We tried in three continents. Here are the results.

Welcome to Birmingham, the friendliest city in the world.

Fresh flowers are everywhere. The road sweepers carry tourist information so they can tell you what's on at the theatre. The taxi drivers are learning languages. Because one year's visitors are worth a billion pounds, the city wants to offer the finest service in the world.

But we are not visitors. We are in Currys, the electrical shop, trying to buy a washing machine. The assistant is explaining why it cannot be delivered at a convenient time. His eyes, which look somewhere else, are bored. "The drivers make their own schedules," he says. "We can't tell them what to do. If we said a specific time for you, we'd have to do the same for everyone."

So is Britain really bad at service? Last week we carried out an informal survey across the world.

Here are some of the findings from a variety of tasks. They reflect the expectations and temperaments of the countries concerned.

Task: in a typical restaurant, change your entire order after five minutes (even if the food has already arrived).

Tokyo: Waiter grimaced slightly (more in concern than annoyance), excused himself and hurried off. Returned a few minutes later with the amended order.

Los Angeles: Waitress, an actress, cracks jokes about pasta being bad for the waistline, and takes fresh order without irritation.

Birmingham: Performed with a smile (at Jeffersons in Hagley Road). When the vegetable dip arrived and our reporter said he wanted a cheese and bacon boat instead, the replacement was served within minutes. "No problem at all," said waitress Sarah Lowe. "And of course you won't have to pay for the dip – our aim is to please."

Buy some shopping in a busy supermarket. Queue. Discover you do not have enough money and ask to put some items back.

Rome: Cashier has no reaction and does not look at customer. Cancels bill and starts again, omitting one item. When customer apologises profusely, replies with neutral voice: "It was no problem."

Tokyo: Cashier polite. No sense of recrimination. In fact, no real reaction at all.

Los Angeles: No problem. Supermarkets are open 24 hours a day, seven days a week. In Von's supermarkets, which have a policy of opening a new till whenever three people queue, the 20,000 staff are trained to listen, nod and make eye contact. "It also comes in useful in their private lives," the store says.

London: (at Sainsbury's, Nine Elms). Cashier, unfazed, smiles and offers to place shopping in cold store, allowing reporter to return later with cash, or deduct some items if he wishes. But the queues are 10 minutes

SERVICE WITHOUT A SMILE

long and 16 of the 37 tills are unattended.

Ask for another counter to be opened to shorten the lunchtime queue at the bank.

Los Angeles: Wells Fargo promises to credit $5 to your account if there are more than two in the queue, whatever the time of day.

Rome: Three of the six tellers' windows unmanned. One teller on the telephone and when he finishes conversation, hangs a sign: "Window non-operative". Reporter told he cannot make a deposit because the computer is down, and bank shuts in five minutes (at 1.30pm). User asks if deposit can be done by hand. Teller panics, suspecting reporter to be a lunatic, but eventually agrees.

Tokyo: Even a simple transaction can take half an hour or more, because everything is processed with customer present. People with legitimate inquiries treated poorly by Western standards, because banking is regarded as above question. Neither friendly nor efficient.

Birmingham: (Barclays, Colmore Row). All tills open except the "quick service" counter. Lengthy queue. Response to reporter's request to open remaining counter: "Sorry, we haven't got any staff available at the moment."

Order a washing machine and ask for delivery between noon and 2pm on Monday.

Tokyo: Shop offers 10% discount and will deliver at any specifed time during opening hours (from 9am to 8pm).

Los Angeles: (Sears Roebuck, America's largest department store group). Breathless

man, sounding harassed, answers washer department's direct line and replies: "Don't deliver Sunday 'n' Monday only Tuesday to Saturday 8 to 12, 12 to 5, 6 to 9. I can guarantee delivery within those three times but not outside them."

Birmingham: (Currys). Evidently well-rehearsed monologue about how delivery time could not be specified or guaranteed, just morning or afternoon.

Glasgow: (Clydesdale, Great Western Road). Could not even say whether morning or afternoon, must stay in all day.

Comet in Dumbarton Road was better: Could not deliver on Monday, only Tuesday – or on Sunday.

How long must you wait to have a telephone installed? Can it be done between noon and 2pm on Monday?

Tokyo: From four days to one week. No.

Rome: Depends on where you live and who you know. For some (with friends) it's a week; for others (in the central district) a year. This year the telephone company promised that the delay would be brought down to three months, but that claim is unproven. No.

Birmingham: At least eight days "to process the application". (In some parts of London, however, it can take months.) No.

Los Angeles: "Hello, it's Linda, how may I help you?" Reporter asks for telephone between noon and 2pm. "Which Monday? We can connect you as soon as you want, but we only guarantee 8am to noon or noon to 5pm. But if you want it close to 2pm I'm sure the installation department will try."

Drive into a petrol station and ask to have your windscreen cleaned, tyre pressure and oil checked.

Tokyo: It is normal in Japan for petrol station attendants to clean windscreens and empty ashtrays without being asked. Oil and tyres checked efficiently.

Rome: Windscreens are cleaned by hundreds of Polish refugees awaiting immigration papers.

Birmingham: At the Mobil "service" station on Stratford Road, the assistant looks astonished. Jokes: "Have you got a disabled sticker then?"

Paper 2 – Writing

Part I

1 You work for an international hotel which would like to attract more English guests. As an English speaker, you have been asked by the Public Relations Manager to help produce a new publicity leaflet in English.

Read the extract from the Public Relations Manager's memo and the current publicity information, with the additional notes. Then, **using the information carefully**, write the text for the new leaflet and the memo as instructed below.

> MEMO
> FROM : Paul Marsden, Public Relations Manager

> Where I'd like your help is with the new publicity leaflet. The current information sheet has the basic facts, but it's very brief and it's also a bit out of date now – I've made a note of changes which should be incorporated. Could you rewrite it in more detail and in a way that catches people's attention and really <u>sells</u> the hotel? One other point – we'll need some new photographs – the current ones are pretty dull. Could you send a memo to Paul B, the hotel photographer, and ask him to take some new shots (in <u>colour</u>) which will do the hotel more justice? Maybe you could also make a few suggestions as to suitable locations for these, e.g. the restaurant or gardens? If you could have the new text on my desk by Monday, I'd appreciate it.
>
> Many thanks,
>
> P

Now write:

a) a **publicity leaflet** (approximately 200 words);
b) an appropriate **memo** to the hotel photographer (approximately 50 words).

You should use your own words as far as possible.

Part 2

Choose **one** of the following writing tasks. Your answer should follow exactly the instructions given. Write approximately 250 words.

2 An English friend is going to spend a weekend in a town or city you know well. This is part of a letter which you receive.

> I'm hoping you can give me some practical advice about where to go and what to see in my short stay. And also what <u>not</u> to do and where <u>not</u> to go – the tourist traps to avoid, etc. Are there any local specialities I should try when I'm eating out? Oh, and what will the weather be like? Let me know if I need to pack sunglasses or an extra sweater!

Write a **letter**.

3 Your school or college has an English Circle which meets once a week but attendance has been poor lately and the meetings may have to end unless new members can be found. You have been asked to write an article for the students' magazine describing the activities of the group and encouraging new members to join.

Write your **article**.

4 You have just seen the following advertisement and have decided to apply.

Do you enjoy travelling?
Do you get on well with children?

Alpha Airlines is looking for responsible young people to act as escorts for children aged between 5 and 12 (individually or in groups of up to six), who are travelling unaccompanied on international flights.

You will need to be level-headed and resourceful.
Some experience of looking after children is essential.

Please write, giving relevant information and saying why you think you would be suitable, to: **Personnel Officer, Alpha Airlines, Huntley.**

Write your **application**.

5 An international English language magazine is planning to have a feature on the subject of humour around the world and you have agreed to contribute a review of the most popular comedy programmes on TV in your country.

Write the **review**.

Paper 3 – English in Use

Part I

For questions **1–15**, read the article below and then decide which word on page **133** best fits each space. Circle the letter you choose for each question. The exercise begins with an example (**0**).

Example: 0 D   0

Flying Pigeons Forever

Bikes are best – in China they are a way of life, at the hub of a wheel that reaches round the Third World.

Pedal, chain, wheels and frame – the basic (0) ... of the bicycle is as near perfect as a machine can be. And bikes are good for you, too. For every person who takes a (1) ... by bike rather than by car there is less pollution, less fuel used, less (2) ... taken on the road and one healthier person.

The world's 800 million bicycles (3) ... cars by two to one and almost half of them are in China. Between them, the 'Flying Pigeon' factory in Tianjin and the 'Forever' factory in Shanghai (4) ... almost seven million bicycles every year. The parts are (5) ... in kit form to be (6) ... by hundreds of local distributors. So employment in the bicycle industry is (7) ... widely across the country. The factory work, though relatively clean and healthy, is (8) ... and unrewarding. Nevertheless, people who work with bicycles seem to share a (9) ... sense of endeavour.

The 'Flying Pigeon' factory exports to 32 countries, particularly to the Third World where sturdy, durable design and low-cost components are (10) ... . China makes all the bicycles sold in Bangladesh, where they are the basic (11) ... of transport for millions of people. Industrial countries have as many bikes per (12) ... as in Asia, but (13) ... to use them less. Tianjin, home of the 'Flying Pigeon', (14) ... the world league, with three-quarters of daily trips made by bike. That may not (15) ... the people of Tianjin the happiest and healthiest in the world – but it should help.

From *The New Internationalist*

0	**A** shape	**B** plan	**C** pattern	Ⓓ design
1	**A** journey	**B** travel	**C** trip	**D** drive
2	**A** area	**B** space	**C** place	**D** distance
3	**A** outnumber	**B** outweigh	**C** overtake	**D** overcome
4	**A** invent	**B** create	**C** process	**D** produce
5	**A** sent for	**B** sent on	**C** sent out	**D** sent in
6	**A** assembled	**B** connected	**C** joined	**D** combined
7	**A** situated	**B** spread	**C** expanded	**D** set
8	**A** recycled	**B** repetitive	**C** recurring	**D** reproduced
9	**A** joint	**B** fellow	**C** common	**D** parallel
10	**A** special	**B** major	**C** key	**D** essential
11	**A** means	**B** medium	**C** way	**D** service
12	**A** man	**B** head	**C** body	**D** hand
13	**A** try	**B** enjoy	**C** require	**D** tend
14	**A** beats	**B** climbs	**C** tops	**D** passes
15	**A** result in	**B** lead to	**C** make	**D** be

Part 2

For questions **16–30**, complete the following article by writing each missing word in the space provided. **Use only one word for each space.** The exercise begins with an example (**0**).

Example: | 0 | in | | 0 |

Skiing at the limits

Screaming, Jonathan Elabor hurls himself (**0**) .... a straight line down the side of a mountain. (**16**) .... seconds, he is travelling at 209 kilometres an hour. (**17**) .... he can hear is his heart pounding at 210 beats a minute, and the hiss of the air over his skin-tight Lycra suit. "It's like jumping from a high board (**18**) .... knowing whether the water's there at the bottom," he says. Elabor is Britain's number one speed skier – a player in the latest, and (**19**) .... say craziest, addition (**20**) .... the winter sports scene.

The speed skier (**21**) .... plunging down a kilometre or more of a mountainside faster than a free-falling parachutist. He's heading (**22**) .... a 100-metre-long timed stretch where radar guns (**23**) .... measure his speed as he flashes by in less than a second. The record, (**24**) .... by Monaco's Michael Prufer, is 228 kilometres an hour – which is more than twice as fast as the legal speed limit (**25**) .... travelling inside the protective steel cage of a car in the UK.

Speed skiing, (**26**) .... motor racing, is a sport driven by technology. In fact, the technology is similar – (**27**) .... use advanced materials developed for (**28**) .... aerospace business, and aerodynamics carefully researched in wind tunnels. (**29**) .... , speed skiers are not surrounded by a million-pound car and a huge team of engineers. They're (**30**) .... their own.

From *Focus* magazine

Part 3

In **most** lines of the following text there is **one** unnecessary word. It is either grammatically incorrect or does not fit in with the sense of the text. For each numbered line **31–46**, write the **unnecessary** word in the spaces next to the question number below. Some lines are correct. Indicate these lines with a tick (✓). The exercise begins with two examples (**0**).

Examples:

0	to		0
0	✓		0

HOW TO HAVE A BABY AND SAVE YOUR CAREER

0   Britain's businesswomen have been told they must to nurse

0   their careers along with their babies if they want to get to the top.

31 The advice which came from a panel of top women executives

32 at a London seminar on the women at work. Businesswomen were

33 advised to keep a high profile while on maternity leave if they

34 wanted to hold on to their jobs. They should be keep in regular

35 touch with their bosses while looking after their babies. Eve

36 Newbold, one of the speakers, said: "One woman on a maternity

37 leave phones me up every week and tells me if she wants her

38 job back. That makes it much harder for anyone not to forget her."

39 The seminar, had entitled "Danger! Women at Work" and

40 attended by more than 300 businesswomen, was told that women

41 must have a major change in attitude if they were able to stand

42 a chance of winning for the battle of the sexes at work. The panel

43 was called for the responsibility of raising children to be shared

44 more equally between the sexes. Catherine James, a director at

45 Grand Metropolitan, said: "Why is the child care such a female

46 issue? We will not solve the problem until men are start to ask

the same questions as we do."

---

31 ....   35 ....   39 ....   43 ....

32 ....   36 ....   40 ....   44 ....

33 ....   37 ....   41 ....   45 ....

34 ....   38 ....   42 ....   46 ....

Part 4

For questions **47–61** read the two texts below. Use the words in the boxes to the right of the texts, listed **47–61**, to form a word that fits in the same numbered space in the text. The exercise begins with an example (**0**).

Example: | **0** | identifiable | | **0** ☐☐

The Breaker, by Minette Walters

There is no such thing as a typical, immediately (**0**) ... Minette Walters book. She has no regular characters, no unique stylistic features, no recurring subjects. No only first-division crime (**47**) ... , in such a short career, has written with such thematic (**48**) ... . The other factors that unite her works are her preference for dark psychological (**49**) ... ; and their (**50**) ... . *The Breaker*, at one level, is a top class murder mystery. It is also a disturbing examination of psychosis. (**51**) ... , Walters avoids the usual array of possible killers. There are just two realistic suspects, and almost to the final page of this (**52**) ... book, the police – and the reader – veer between them as new (**53**) ... pile up.

(**0**)	IDENTIFY
(**47**)	NOVEL
(**48**)	VARY
(**49**)	PERCEIVE
(**50**)	EXCELLENT
(**51**)	COURAGE
(**52**)	ABSORB
(**53**)	REVEAL

Louis Pasteur, by Patrice Debre

Patrice Debre is himself a physician and immunologist, and his biography is an account, clearly and unpretentiously written, of Pasteur's (**54**) ... scientific (**55**) ... . How can these be explained? One does not find in Pasteur that extraordinary fully-formed talent that brilliant (**56**) ... or physicists have. He even failed some exams in his youth (there is therefore hope for us all). His genius was more an infinite capacity for taking pains. An example of this is his (**57**) ... of anaerobes, the bacteria that flourish only in the (**58**) ... of oxygen. One day he noticed, while looking down his microscope, that bacteria at the edges of a smear on a slide were (**59**) ... , while those at the centre were highly active. This is the kind of small (**60**) ... which the vast majority of us would have (**61**) ... .

(**54**)	NUMBER
(**55**)	ACHIEVE
(**56**)	MATHEMATICS
(**57**)	DISCOVER
(**58**)	ABSENT
(**59**)	MOBILE
(**60**)	OBSERVE
(**61**)	LOOK

---

47 ....
48 ....
49 ....
50 ....
51 ....

52 ....
53 ....
54 ....
55 ....
56 ....

57 ....
58 ....
59 ....
60 ....
61 ....

Part 5

For questions **62–74**, read the following informal note and use the information to complete the numbered gaps in the letter to your landlord. **Use no more than two words** for each gap. The words which you need **do not occur** in the informal note. The exercise begins with an example (**0**).

Example: | **0** | inform you | ☐ 0 ☐ |

INFORMAL NOTE

Dear Sarah,

Just a note to let you know my new address, though I'm afraid it may be a temporary one! My brother fixed up this accommodation for me while I was away, as you know, but I don't suppose he had time to look the place over very thoroughly and of course the landlord didn't mention any problems! Anyway, it was quite a shock when I arrived – the carpet in the living room is dirty and stained, one of the kitchen taps drips all the time, a window pane is broken and, worst of all, there's a smell of gas from the cooker, which could be really dangerous. I'm writing to the landlord to let him know what's wrong, and ask him to sort things out as soon as possible. If he won't agree, the only thing I can do is contact the local council. Wish me luck!

Love,

H

FORMAL LETTER

Dear Mr Stubbs,

Top Floor Flat, 25 St Helen's Road

I have recently moved into the above property and I'm writing to
(**0**) .... of a number of problems which require urgent
(**62**) .... Although my brother (**63**) .... the flat
on my (**64**) .... , he obviously wasn't (**65**) ....
these problems and, if they had been (**66**) .... out to him,
he certainly would not have signed the rental agreement.
The two most important problems are the gas cooker, which appears to have a gas
(**67**) .... and therefore represents a potentially serious
(**68**) .... hazard, and a broken window pane which needs
(**69**) .... for reasons of security. In addition, the carpet in the living
room needs (**70**) .... , and there is also a tap in the kitchen which
drips (**71**) ....
I trust you will (**72**) .... the necessary repairs without
(**73**) .... If not, I will have no (**74**) .... but to
contact the local council.
Yours sincerely.

137

Part 6

For questions **75–80**, read through the following text and then choose from the list **A–J** the best phrase given below it to fill each of the spaces. Write one letter (**A–J**) in each space provided. **Some of the suggested answers do not fit at all**. The exercise begins with an example (**0**).

Example:

Adapting to the climate – cold comforts and hot sweats

From the poles to the tropics, weather determines the way we live. Most cultures have developed technology to conquer the elements – using clothing, housing and food (**0**) ... . Eskimos have learned to cope with temperatures that drop to –50°C. They pile on layers of clothes and retreat to the insulation of their igloos (**75**) ... .

The average Eskimo has a metabolic rate 30 per cent higher than the average European. But this is the result of a diet low in carbohydrates and high in protein and fat – (**76**) ... . It is quickly lost if the diet is changed. Eskimos have also evolved short arms and legs so they have less surface area to radiate heat. People (**77**) ... who are acclimatised to heat have a larger blood volume, enabling them to radiate heat more effectively. In a hot dry climate sweating is the best way for the body (**78**) ... . But in the tropics, where there is high humidity, increasing sweat production may offer no advantage (**79**) ... . Acclimatisation to heat encourages a tendency for salt concentrations in sweat to decrease. Nigerians, for example, lose significantly less salt (**80**) ... than British men. This specific adaptation to the climate is due to increases in the concentration of a hormone called aldosterone in the blood, which acts on the sweat glands and the kidneys to aid conservation of salt.

From *Focus* magazine

A through sweating

B helping them to work more efficiently

C not because they were born with this advantage

D because sweat does not evaporate

E to reduce their body temperature

F for warmth

G living in the tropics

H by dressing up warmly

I to lose excess heat

J to adapt to extremes of climate

Paper 4 – Listening

Part I

You will hear an advertisement for a sale of household equipment.
For questions **1–10**, fill in the missing information.

You will hear the recording twice.

Product	Sale Price	Features	Special Offer
Colour TV	£499	51 cm screen + [____ **1**]	Free [____ **2**]
[____ **3**]	£369	12 place settings	[____ **4**]
Cooker	£649	[____ **5**] + ceramic hob	Chance to win [____ **6**]
Chest freezer	£369	[____ **7**] model	Free [____ **8**]
[____ **9**]	£99	Built-in tools	Free [____ **10**]

139

Part 2

You will hear some advice on complaining about a holiday. As you listen, complete the information for questions 11–18.

Listen very carefully as you will hear the recording ONCE only.

HOLIDAY COMPLAINTS

While you're away …

- Try to sort out any problems at the time by making a complaint to the company [_____ **11**]

- Remember to take the holiday brochure and a copy of the [_____ **12**] with you.

- Take photos of the things you're complaining about, e.g. [_____ **13**] of your room.

- Keep receipts for any money you spend to [_____ **14**] the problems.

- The company will find it more difficult to ignore a complaint which is [_____ **15**] by several people.

- Complete the tour operator's complaint form and remember to keep [_____ **16**] of it.

When you return …

- Write to the company quickly, saying how much [_____ **17**] you require.

- If you're still not satisfied, use ABTA's independent arbitration scheme for a [_____ **18**] of about £30.

Part 3

You will hear part of an interview with Mary Dallas, an archaeologist whose work involves studying aboriginal sites in Australia. For questions **19–30** complete each of the statements.

You will hear the recording twice.

Mary's work involves working out in the bush and also sitting **19**

She works away from her office for about **20** of her time.

She looks for aboriginal sites in areas which are unaffected by **21** , suburbs or industry.

She decides whether to go out alone depending on how or **22** it's likely to be.

In certain types of country, there's a risk of **23** or falling down a cliff.

Among the animals she might see are different types of **24**

She first wanted to be an archaeologist when she was **25**

In the beginning she was mainly interested in **26** archaeology.

She became fascinated with aboriginal culture while she was **27**

Mary wishes her degree studies had included more **28** subjects.

The anthropology course at Sydney University used to have the nickname **29**

Things have changed in that nowadays more archaeological students are **30**

Part 4

You will hear five short extracts in which various people are talking about speeches they have heard.

TASK ONE

For questions **31–35**, match the extracts as you hear them with the occasions when the speeches were made, listed **A–H**.

A a meeting for women

B a birthday party

C a debate

D a wedding

E a competition

F a party for someone who was leaving

G a prize-giving ceremony

H a school meeting

| 31 |
| 32 |
| 33 |
| 34 |
| 35 |

TASK TWO

For questions **36–40**, match the extracts as you hear them with the aspects of the speeches that were impressive, listed **A–H**.

A It was amusing.

B It was strongly felt.

C It contained a lot of useful facts.

D It was a good story.

E It touched the emotions.

F It was delivered without notes.

G It led to a lot of questions.

H It included practical demonstrations.

| 36 |
| 37 |
| 38 |
| 39 |
| 40 |

Remember that you must complete both tasks as you listen.
You will hear the recording twice.

Paper 5 – Speaking

Work in groups of three. One student should play the role of the examiner, giving instructions, asking further questions and making sure both candidates play an equal part in the conversation.

Part 1 (3 minutes) Introductions and General Social Conversation

Imagine you had never met your partner.

- Greet the examiner and introduce your partner to them.

- Find out whether your partner enjoys cooking and what his/her particular likes and dislikes in food are. Tell the others about your tastes in food.

- Tell the others what kind of music you like and whether you play any kind of musical instrument. Find out about your partner's musical tastes.

- Ask your partner about their future plans and ambitions. Explain what yours are.

Part 2 (3 or 4 minutes)

In this part of the test you will each have the opportunity to talk for a minute.

Task 1

Rooms (Describe and compare)

You will each have the same pair of pictures to look at.

Turn to the pictures on page 152.

Candidate A: Talk about both the pictures to your partner, commenting on the similarities and differences, and saying whether you enjoy visiting places like these. You have about a minute for this.

Candidate B: Listen carefully to your partner's description. When A has finished, you can mention anything he/she has omitted. What pictures do you have on your wall?

Task 2

Boats (Describe and identify)

You will each have a set of pictures showing boats. Don't look at each other's pictures.

Candidate B: Turn to the pictures on page 154. Choose two pictures and describe them so that your partner can identify them. You have about one minute for this.

Candidate A: Turn to the pictures on page 153. Listen carefully to your partner's description and decide which two pictures are being described. If you still need help at the end, you can ask your partner one or two questions. Which of the pictures do you like best? Why?

Part 3 (3 or 4 minutes)

Cartoon (Exchange opinions)

In this part of the test you have to discuss a topic with your partner.

Look at the cartoon below and decide what point the cartoonist is making. Discuss what solution there could be to the problem and talk about other sources of noise in modern life which cause problems.

You have three or four minutes for this.

Part 4 (3 or 4 minutes)

In this part of the test you and your partner have to report on the outcome of your discussion in Part 3, saying whether you agreed or not. You then take part in a more general discussion on the topic with your partner and the examiner.

Practise your reporting and discussion skills by working with another pair. Take it in turns to summarise and explain the conclusions you reached, and then discuss the following questions:

Do you think traffic should be banned from city centres?

• Should we stop building new roads altogether?

• How can people be encouraged to make more use of public transport?

• What kinds of noise do you find most annoying?

• What would you do if your neighbour's loud music was keeping you awake?

• Is there anything you do which creates a noise other people might find annoying?

Test 1, Paper 5 • Part 2 Task 1 • **A**

Test 1, Paper 5 • Part 2 Task 1 • **B**

Test 1, Paper 5 • Part 2 Task 2 • **A**

Test 1, Paper 5 • Part 2 Task 2 • **B**

Test 2, Paper 5 • Part 2 • **B**

Test 3, Paper 5 • Part 2 Task 1

Test 2, Paper 5 • Part 3

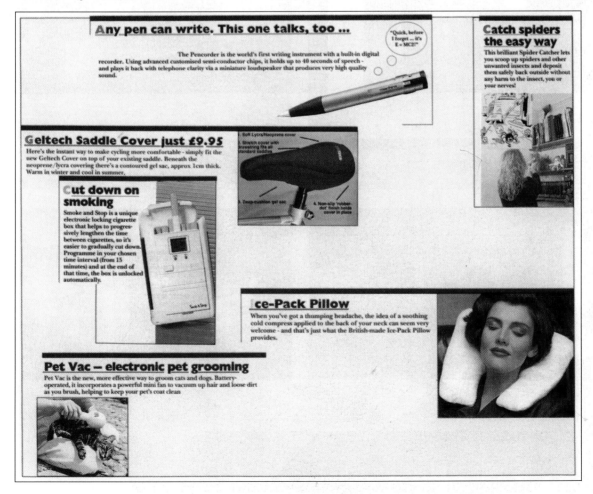

Test 3, Paper 5 • Part 2 Task 2 • **A**

Test 2, Paper 5 • Part 2 • **A**

Test 3, Paper 5 • Part 2 Task 2 • **B**

Test 4, Paper 5 • Part 2 Task 1 • **A**

149

Test 4, Paper 5 • Part 2 Task 1 • **B**

Test 4, Paper 5 • Part 2 Task 2 • **A**

Test 4, Paper 5 • Part 2 Task 2 • **B**

Test 5, Paper 5 • Part 2 Task 1 • **A**

Test 5, Paper 5 • Part 2 Task 1 • **B**

Test 5, Paper 5 • Part 2 Task 2 • **A**

Test 5, Paper 5 • Part 2 Task 2 • **B**

SAMPLE

Candidate Name
If not already printed, write name
in CAPITALS and complete the
Candidate No. grid (in pencil).
Candidate's signature --

Examination Title

Centre

Supervisor:
[X] If the candidate is ABSENT or has WITHDRAWN shade here ⬚

Centre No.

Candidate No.

Examination Details

0	0	0	0
1	1	1	1
2	2	2	2
3	3	3	3
4	4	4	4
5	5	5	5
6	6	6	6
7	7	7	7
8	8	8	8
9	9	9	9

Multiple-choice Answer Sheet

Use a pencil   Mark one letter for each question.

For example:

If you think C is the right answer to the
question, mark your answer sheet like this: 0 | A B C

Change your answer
like this:

1	A B C D E F G H I
2	A B C D E F G H I
3	A B C D E F G H I
4	A B C D E F G H I
5	A B C D E F G H I
6	A B C D E F G H I
7	A B C D E F G H I
8	A B C D E F G H I
9	A B C D E F G H I
10	A B C D E F G H I
11	A B C D E F G H I
12	A B C D E F G H I
13	A B C D E F G H I
14	A B C D E F G H I
15	A B C D E F G H I
16	A B C D E F G H I
17	A B C D E F G H I
18	A B C D E F G H I
19	A B C D E F G H I
20	A B C D E F G H I

21	A B C D E F G H I
22	A B C D E F G H I
23	A B C D E F G H I
24	A B C D E F G H I
25	A B C D E F G H I
26	A B C D E F G H I
27	A B C D E F G H I
28	A B C D E F G H I
29	A B C D E F G H I
30	A B C D E F G H I
31	A B C D E F G H I
32	A B C D E F G H I
33	A B C D E F G H I
34	A B C D E F G H I
35	A B C D E F G H I
36	A B C D E F G H I
37	A B C D E F G H I
38	A B C D E F G H I
39	A B C D E F G H I
40	A B C D E F G H I

41	A B C D E F G H I
42	A B C D E F G H I
43	A B C D E F G H I
44	A B C D E F G H I
45	A B C D E F G H I
46	A B C D E F G H I
47	A B C D E F G H I
48	A B C D E F G H I
49	A B C D E F G H I
50	A B C D E F G H I
51	A B C D E F G H I
52	A B C D E F G H I
53	A B C D E F G H I
54	A B C D E F G H I
55	A B C D E F G H I
56	A B C D E F G H I
57	A B C D E F G H I
58	A B C D E F G H I
59	A B C D E F G H I
60	A B C D E F G H I

UNIVERSITY of CAMBRIDGE
Local Examinations Syndicate

SAMPLE

Candidate Name
If not already printed, write name in CAPITALS and complete the Candidate No. grid (in pencil).

Candidate's signature

Examination Title

Centre

Supervisor:

[X] If the candidate is ABSENT or has WITHDRAWN shade here ▭

Centre No.

Candidate No.

Examination Details

0	0	0	0
1	1	1	1
2	2	2	2
3	3	3	3
4	4	4	4
5	5	5	5
6	6	6	6
7	7	7	7
8	8	8	8
9	9	9	9

Candidate Answer Sheet

Use a pencil

For Parts 1 and 6:
Mark ONE letter for each question.
For example, if you think **B** is the right answer to the question, mark your answer sheet like this:

| 0 | A B̲ C D |

For Parts 2, 3, 4 and 5:
Write your answers in the spaces next to the numbers like this:

| 0 | example |

Part 1				
1	A	B	C	D
2	A	B	C	D
3	A	B	C	D
4	A	B	C	D
5	A	B	C	D
6	A	B	C	D
7	A	B	C	D
8	A	B	C	D
9	A	B	C	D
10	A	B	C	D
11	A	B	C	D
12	A	B	C	D
13	A	B	C	D
14	A	B	C	D
15	A	B	C	D

Part 2	Do not write here
16	16
17	17
18	18
19	19
20	20
21	21
22	22
23	23
24	24
25	25
26	26
27	27
28	28
29	29
30	30

Turn over for parts 3 - 6 →

SAMPLE

Part 3		Do not write here
31		31
32		32
33		33
34		34
35		35
36		36
37		37
38		38
39		39
40		40
41		41
42		42
43		43
44		44
45		45
46		46

Part 5		Do not write here
62		62
63		63
64		64
65		65
66		66
67		67
68		68
69		69
70		70
71		71
72		72
73		73
74		74

Part 4		Do not write here
47		47
48		48
49		49
50		50
51		51
52		52
53		53
54		54
55		55
56		56
57		57
58		58
59		59
60		60
61		61

Part 6									
75	A	B	C	D	E	F	G	H	I
76	A	B	C	D	E	F	G	H	I
77	A	B	C	D	E	F	G	H	I
78	A	B	C	D	E	F	G	H	I
79	A	B	C	D	E	F	G	H	I
80	A	B	C	D	E	F	G	H	I

UNIVERSITY of CAMBRIDGE
Local Examinations Syndicate

SAMPLE

Candidate Name
If not already printed, write name
in CAPITALS and complete the
Candidate No. grid (in pencil).

Candidate's signature

Examination Title

Centre

Supervisor:

[X] If the candidate is ABSENT or has WITHDRAWN shade here ▭

Centre No.

Candidate No.

Examination Details

0	0	0	0
1	1	1	1
2	2	2	2
3	3	3	3
4	4	4	4
5	5	5	5
6	6	6	6
7	7	7	7
8	8	8	8
9	9	9	9

Listening Comprehension Answer Sheet

Enter the test number here ▯▯▯

For office use only [3] CPE [5] CAE [0][1][2][3][4][5][6][7][8][9]
[0][1][2][3][4][5][6][7][8][9]

Write your answers below	Do not write here	Continue here	Do not write here
1	1	21	21
2	2	22	22
3	3	23	23
4	4	24	24
5	5	25	25
6	6	26	26
7	7	27	27
8	8	28	28
9	9	29	29
10	10	30	30
11	11	31	31
12	12	32	32
13	13	33	33
14	14	34	34
15	15	35	35
16	16	36	36
17	17	37	37
18	18	38	38
19	19	39	39
20	20	40	40

158

©UCLES 1999   Photocopiable

▶ Tapescripts

Test 1

There are four parts 1, 2, 3 and 4. You will hear Part 2 once only. All the other parts of the test will be heard twice. There will be a pause before each part to allow you to look through the questions and other pauses to let you think about your answers.

You should write your answers on the question paper. In the exam you will have ten minutes at the end to transfer your answers to the separate answer sheet.

Part 1

You will hear some information about home security. For questions 1–9, fill in the missing information. You will hear the recording twice.

Thank you for calling the Goldmark Insurance Telephone Advice Line on home security. I'm Jeremy Kent, customer services manager at Goldmark Insurance, and I'm here with some tips to help you guard against intruders.

The first line of defence is obviously the doors, **all** the doors, not just the front door. Many houses have door locks which are cheap or flimsy and can be easily opened, so make sure you fit strong, good quality locks to all your outside doors.

Next the windows. Downstairs windows are one of the burglar's favourite methods of entry because they often allow him easy access. Again, the solution is to fit strong window locks and there are many different types on the market. This way, even if the burglar breaks a pane of glass, he won't be able to reach in and open the window from the inside.

Upstairs windows may seem less accessible but not so in the case of the determined burglar because he can get to them from the roof or with a ladder. Once again, secure all upstairs windows with strong locks.

There is a type of window which is the burglar's particular favourite and that's the louvre window. These are most often found in bathrooms and kitchens and they consist of several panels of glass. The problem is that the glass panels slide out. So they're an invitation to a burglar, and if you have any windows of that type, the best advice is to fit a lock or, better still, fit ordinary windows instead.

The next area to consider is the garage or the garden shed. They're both handy places to keep tools in and that means that they can be a handy source of equipment for burglars too. There's many a burglar who has been grateful to the householder for this assistance. Fit a good padlock on the door or remove your tools.

Finally, the porch. If there is no light, as is often the case, it means that visitors can't be identified. You have to open the door before you know who it is that's calling, and then it may be too late. You should buy a special security light which is designed to switch on as soon as anyone approaches your front door, even before they ring the doorbell. It's often enough to scare away a potential thief.

Thank you for calling the Goldmark Insurance Advice Line on home security.

You will now hear the recording again.

That is the end of Part 1.

Part 2

You will hear about a competition for young writers. As you listen, complete the information for questions 10–17. Listen very carefully as you will hear the recording once only.

Now to that competition I mentioned at the beginning of the programme. I'll be giving you details about how to enter in a minute, so have a pencil and a piece of paper ready. The Bookworm Young Writers' Competition is open to anyone aged 16 or under on the closing date – and I'll tell you when that is later. There are more than fifty prizes and the winning entries will have their work published in a paperback book next year.

So how do you enter? Well, you can submit any original piece of writing whether it's poetry, prose, or even drama. But it must be original. Anything which is a copy or a near copy of something you've read elsewhere will be automatically disqualified. The maximum length for each entry is 3,500 words but, of course, you don't **have** to write that much or anything like it.

Now, this part is important. Your entry must be accompanied by a signed statement from one of your parents or from your teacher saying that your entry is all your own work and that it was written unaided, that is without any help from anyone. Now, don't forget to get that statement and make sure it's signed.

If you need to use more than one sheet of paper, make sure the sheets are all clearly numbered and also pinned together. You don't want your brilliant entry coming adrift! When you've got your entry ready, you'll need to send it to: Young Writers' Competition, PO Box 2000, Taunton, Somerset, TA1 5QT. Oh, and remember to keep a copy of your work because none of the entries will be returned.

And now that all-important closing date. All entries must be received by September 12th, so you've got a whole month to work on your entry. Get writing, and good luck!

That is the end of Part 2.

Part 3

You will hear an interview with Robert Miles who works as a Flight Service Director for an airline. For questions 18–29 complete each of the statements. You will hear the recording twice.

Interviewer Robert, can I ask you what the good parts of the job are?

Robert Miles Well, the good parts are the travelling to different areas of the world and looking after different people on board the aircraft.

Interviewer And what about the bad parts? Are they looking after not so nice people?

Robert Miles No, no, no that's part and parcel of the job. You've got to adapt to looking after good people as well as bad people. I guess the bad part would be the long hours that are involved. We do up to sixteen, seventeen hours at a time – that's probably the hardest part.

Interviewer And how long have you been doing this job?

Robert Miles I've been with the company for twenty-six years.

Interviewer Goodness! And how did you actually come to start your career?

Robert Miles I used to work in the public service. And at that time, the recruitment of flight attendants was, was very much word of mouth, and one of the guys in the office applied for the job and didn't get it. And he said to me that they were looking for, well, for people of lesser intelligence so I applied for the job! And I managed to get it and I've, well, it's been great. I've never looked back.

Interviewer You've never been tempted to leave or do something else?

Robert Miles Well, like everybody else I decided I'd do it for two years initially, to see the world. But once you get bitten by the bug, that's it; you never seem to get rid of it. And I've never wanted to leave.

Interviewer So, how much time do you spend now, say, in a month actually flying?

Robert Miles Well, what we have is a bid period – that's a working period of fifty-six days and you must have a minimum of eighteen days off in fifty-six. But the system's pretty complicated and it works out in hours. You can have up to twenty-eight days off in a working period if things work out right.

Interviewer And you spend some time behind a desk as well?

Robert Miles Yes. Yes, I'm, I'm attached to Cabin Crew Management – have been for the last three years. It's good because it gives you a chance to see what goes on behind the scenes, particularly with the Customer Relations Department but, but other departments as well. Whereas the normal crew that fly, continually fly, they never get a chance to see what goes on behind the scenes.

Interviewer Have you ever had as a passenger anyone particularly famous?

Robert Miles Yes. Yes, I've been lucky enough to be a crew member on two royal flights. I think it was about '73. I managed to do two sectors with the Queen. We brought her out of Vancouver to Honolulu and then from Singapore to Teheran. That was sensational.

Interviewer And what do you do when you get somebody who's really frightened of flying?

Robert Miles I think the easiest thing is to reassure them that air travel is probably the safest way to go. I guess you've got more chance of having an accident if you walk across the road. If you can reassure the passenger and stay with them as much as you can, show them how the aircraft works, take them on the flight deck, let them see what the captain does, what the flight deck crew do. And then explain that the cabin crew are fully trained in safety procedures on board the aircraft, and if anything is going to happen, they're in safe hands.

Interviewer You've said that it's your job to look after all kinds of passengers, the agreeable ones and the disagreeable ones, but what would you say is the most annoying thing from your point of view in a passenger?

Robert Miles I guess a passenger who makes completely unreasonable demands, things that just can't be done on board the aircraft. We always try to help passengers in any way. But there are some passengers who want the impossible. I mean, if we could give them the aircraft they'd probably take it!

Interviewer You've been doing this job for a long time. What have been the biggest changes in that time in the nature of your work?

Robert Miles Well I started off on 707 aircraft. And now we're up to the big 747 400 series which carry over 400 people. In the early days the maximum we carried was 140 and we could give a more personalised service to the passengers then. We had a lot more time to talk to people individually. And now it's more of a group discussion where you talk to six or seven people in a row at one time. That's probably the biggest change. And another is flying longer sectors. You know, I mean, we now operate from Bangkok straight through to London; we operate Sydney–Los Angeles direct. I mean, they're the big changes.

Interviewer Robert, thanks very much.

Robert Miles Oh, great.

You will now hear the recording again.

That is the end of Part 3.

Part 4

You will hear five short extracts in which various people are talking about bargains they have bought. Task one. For questions 30–34, match the extracts as you hear them with the things the speakers bought, listed A–H. Task two. For questions 35–39, match the extracts as you hear them with the reasons the original owners sold things cheaply, listed A–H. Remember you must complete both tasks as you listen. You will hear the recording twice.

1

Yes, it's lovely, isn't it? It's a typical oriental design. I love the colour. I think it's hand-made, actually, but I don't suppose it's valuable or anything. I got it from an aunt of mine. It was on the floor in her hallway, and I said how much I liked it. Well, she looked at me as if I was mad and said, 'What that old thing? Well, you can have it if you want.' She said she'd much rather have a nice modern one to go with the wallpaper. So I bought her a new one quite cheaply and kept this, and we're both happy.

2

It belonged to somebody I knew at work. He'd ordered it from a catalogue thinking it would be an easy way to lose weight. But it came in kit form and by the time he got it assembled, he'd sort of gone off the whole idea – he said he'd feel stupid sitting pedalling away at it in front of the television – so he never got round to trying it at all. He let me have it quite reasonably. I think it's great!

3

A friend of mine was going to live abroad and he sold it to me for £50 – he said he didn't have time to put an advert in the paper and all that. I reckon I got a real bargain. That was three years ago and it's been going strong ever since. Not a spot of rust anywhere on the bodywork and the interior is immaculate. The only thing I've had to buy is two new tyres.

4

I was at a jumble sale, wandering around and it caught my eye. I'd been looking for something to put my computer on and it seemed about the right size. It was quite badly scratched but I could see it was beautifully made. If you pull out that drawer in the front, you'll see what I mean. It only cost £10, if I remember rightly. Since then, I've been told it's antique and worth quite a lot more than £10!

5

My brother was having a clear-out and he offered it to me for a fiver. He didn't use it any more – he's got a word processor now – so it was just taking up valuable space. It's not electric or electronic or anything, just a good old-fashioned manual one – but it works really well. My tutor at college is delighted – he says it takes him half the time to read through one of my essays now.

You will now hear the recording again.

That is the end of the test.

Test 2

Part 1

You will hear part of a radio programme about answering machines. For questions 1–9, fill in the missing information. You will hear the recording twice.

Presenter Next up in the programme is our consumer slot and today we take a look at three new answering machines. Here's Penny Kennedy with her report.

Penny Kennedy Having an answering machine means that people can get in touch with you even when

161

you're out, and they're also a handy way of avoiding calls when you're watching your favourite TV programme! Prices vary enormously as do the features which are included, so it's worth comparing models carefully. For example, most machines give you a limited time for the announcement you make, giving your name, telephone number and so on. Of the three models we tested, the **Cuckoo** is the meanest, with only 15 seconds available for the announcement; the **Budgie** has 30, while the top-of-the-range **Vulture** offers a full minute. Most machines also give the caller a maximum time to leave a message. This was the case with the two cheaper models we tested.

After these basics, there are a number of special features which may or may not be useful to you. Most answering machines these days have a remote control feature so you can play back your messages from another phone. The more expensive models also usually have a system for logging the time and date of each message. What else? Yes, you may find it useful to be able to make two-way recordings of conversations if you use your phone for business. So, our verdict on the three answering machines we tested? First, the **Budgie** which, appropriately enough, is a budget model. This performed well in most respects and we think it's good value if you don't need too many features. Next the **Cuckoo** which was a bit more expensive but it's worth paying the extra for longer messages. It's also the only model that can be fixed to the wall – which is good for saving space in a small room. The **Cuckoo** made very clear recordings but we found the instructions for listening to and saving messages rather complicated. Finally the **Vulture** which, at nearly £200, was the most expensive model we tested: this was child's play to use and the recorded messages were crystal-clear. It has all the features you'd ever want and does just about everything except make the tea! Even so, we thought it was a bit over-priced.

Presenter Thanks, Penny, for that report. And I've no doubt there **will** be a model which makes the tea before long ...

You will now hear the recording again.

That is the end of Part 1.

Part 2

You will hear a tour guide giving a group of tourists some extra details about their programme. As you listen, complete the information for questions 10–17. Listen very carefully as you will hear the recording once only.

Hello, everybody. My name is Sally Taylor and on behalf of Goodwill Tours, I'd like to welcome you all to Jordan for your Magic of Petra holiday break.

Well, we'll be setting off shortly for our drive to the hotel and in the meantime I'd like to give you some information about the programme. First of all, the bad news! Because of your late arrival this evening, the welcome dinner which is mentioned on your programme has been cancelled. Now the hotel will be providing sandwiches and fruit though, so if you're feeling peckish don't worry!

Tomorrow morning breakfast will be served by the swimming pool. After that there's a coach tour of the city, and coaches will leave the hotel at 9.30. The afternoon is free for relaxing or shopping, but for the energetic ones amongst you, we've organised an optional visit to the gold market. It's one of the most interesting gold markets in the Middle East, in fact, and well worth seeing. In the evening, although it's not mentioned on your programme, we'll be having a buffet dinner and this will be accompanied by musical entertainment. We hope this will make up for the welcome dinner you're missing tonight. Good.

On Tuesday, you'll need to have an early breakfast because this is the big day and our journey to Petra begins at 8.30. Now it's important to choose comfortable clothing to wear because you'll be spending quite a few hours on the coach and the day also includes some horse-riding, of course! The journey takes about three hours and, after your tour of the city, you'll be lunching at the Petra Vista Hotel. We leave Petra at about 4 o'clock and, on the way back, there's another event that's not on your programme. We'll be making a stop for afternoon tea at a Turkish fort. This is one of several historical Turkish forts in Jordan and it makes a splendid setting for our refreshment stop. In the evening, there's the special 1001 Arabian Nights dinner back at the hotel. That is very special.

Now, are there any questions?

That is the end of Part 2.

Part 3

You will hear an interview with a subeditor on a newspaper. For questions 18–24, choose the correct option from A, B, C or D. You will hear the recording twice.

A So, um, what is it you do?

B Well, I work as a casual subeditor on the finance desk of *The Australian* newspaper. That's the only national daily in Australia. And, er …

A What does 'casual' mean, exactly?

B Well, it means I'm not part of the full-time staff. Quite a big proportion of the subediting staff on newspapers, certainly here, and I think in England as well, are casual employees who work a few days a week. I just do three days a week and I resist all blandishments to do more because, well because I've never liked doing too much of one thing.

A So how long do you do each day?

B You do a full shift …

A Which is how long?

B Which is about seven hours, all told. I don't know if you know what subeditors do? Not everyone does. People often assume that you're sort of the deputy editor, which is a quite different thing. But subeditors get the 'copy', the story, into shape. They have to sort out any problems with the grammar or spelling, for example. Sometimes, depending on the sort of paper you're working for and the sort of report you're working on, you rewrite stories if the reporter's not picked the best angle, or if you're told to take a different angle. You also write the headlines and the captions for pictures, and the 'breakout heads', that's, you know, the little headlines you get in the middle of the article …

A Yes, what's the purpose of those?

B The purpose, really, is just to break up the appearance of the page. If you get, even on a quality like *The Times* or *The Australian*, if you get a solid grey mass of copy, of type, people are deterred from reading it. So they break it up into what looks like bite-sized pieces. The whole business of laying out a page is to do with encouraging people to read it. As indeed is the business of writing headlines and putting pictures in and all that.

A So how does the work go during a shift? Are there periods of boredom and inactivity?

B There have been in the past, but working on the finance desk now on *The Australian*, they've increased the size of 'the book', the section, the finance section. And we now have a lot of foreign stories. So, we work on those first off. You get stuff from *The Economist*, stuff from *The Washington Post*, all sorts of foreign copy. So we'll start at three o'clock in the afternoon, working on that stuff and then we'll work towards the front of our section which will be, I mean, the main front pages will all be Australian stories. And they'll be coming in up to, say, about nine thirty for the first edition.

A And then?

B And then, once the first edition pages are done, we check them, between editions, because we don't have a spell-check programme. It's quite primitive technology. Funnily enough, *News Limited* in Sydney was, if not the first, among the first newspapers in the world to be set up with what's called the new technology, electronic photo typesetting and all the rest of it. But it still has its original equipment from 1977 or something like that, so it's no longer state of the art, I need hardly say. And often there are areas that are not filled in the first edition, and we put in 'house ads', there – what are called house ads, which just means we advertise our own newspaper, you know, we say 'Read Saturday's *Australian* for the property section' or, you know, something along those lines, or 'Motoring on Wednesdays', you know. And then we'll take the house ads out and replace them with news when we get late-breaking stories or late comment from our own correspondents.

A And is it satisfying to see your headlines in the paper the next day?

B It is if they're good, yeah. If you've come up with something really nice. But it's surprising how rarely that happens on a po-faced paper like *The Australian*, because they won't let you go in for all the jokes and the slang that you can use in a tabloid. So they have to be fairly high-brow jokes, you know, they have to be a bit sly.

You will now hear the recording again.

That is the end of Part 3.

Part 4

You will hear five short extracts in which various people are talking about publications they read. Task one. For questions 25–29, match the extracts as you hear them with the publications the speakers read, listed A–H. Task two. For questions 30–34, match the extracts as you hear them with the speakers' favourite features, listed A–H. Remember you must complete both tasks as you listen. You will hear the recording twice.

1

Well, the main point is that it helps you plan your viewing, obviously. But actually, there's a surprising amount in it besides programme listings. Articles about soap stars, background to some of the popular series – quite interesting some of them, sometimes. But what I really like is the crossword, the general knowledge one. There's a £1,000 prize. I haven't won it yet but I live in hope! It's not bad for 60p, is it? Cheaper than a lot of other glossy mags.

2

I wouldn't say it made riveting reading, but it's useful. I mean, you have to keep in touch with what's going on in your field, don't you? They have short pieces about new developments, test reports on new equipment – that sort of thing. But the section I always turn to first, I'm afraid, is the job ads – because I certainly don't intend to be stuck in my current job for the rest of my career. So, I don't think I'd actually go out and buy it, no. But as it's free for union members, I'll give it a read.

3

I used to get a paper delivered every day but not anymore. They take up such a lot of time, don't they? And you get all the important news on the telly anyway. Now I just buy one on Sunday. It makes sense because you tend to get more in-depth articles, articles which go into the week's events quite thoroughly, I mean. And there's more time to really read and enjoy them at the weekend. It works out at quite a saving too, you know, cancelling the daily. That's another advantage.

4

It often comes with a free gift like a CD or a gadget for the hi-fi system, which is fun. And then every month they feature a different composer and tell you all about their life and work and so on, though I don't always have time to read the whole article. But I do make a point of reading up about the latest recordings – seeing what the experts think – because I'm trying to build up a serious CD collection, and I only want the best. It costs £3, but I think it's well worth the price.

5

Most of it's rubbish, yeah. Loads of ads and boring stories about some school pupil winning a prize, or some old couple's 50th wedding anniversary. A waste of money really. The only reason I bother to

get it really is to check the football results, and see if there's any news about City – because I reckon I'm their biggest supporter. Then, apart from having a quick look at the entertainments page, and seeing if there's anything of interest on TV, the whole thing goes in the bin.

You will now hear the recording again.

That is the end of the test.

Test 3
Part 1

You will hear some information about places to visit in the historic harbour area of the City of Bristol. For questions 1–10, fill in the missing information. You will hear the recording twice.

Welcome to Bristol's historic harbour area. In the eighteenth century, Bristol was the leading English city and port outside London. Nowadays, the harbour is no longer used for commercial shipping and it has been redeveloped as a centre for leisure activities and water sports. As you walk around, however, you will see evidence of the harbour's history in the many waterside buildings.

One example, close to the city centre, is the Watershed. In Victorian times this was used as a storage shed but it has now been imaginatively redeveloped as a media centre with two cinemas, a gallery and photographic studios.

If you cross to the opposite quayside, you'll come to the Arnolfini. It's now an important arts centre, which is well-known for its exhibitions of modern art, but in the last century it was a tea warehouse.

A few minutes' walk from the Arnolfini is the *Thekla*, an old boat which has found a new use. This was once a freight steamer but it's been converted into an entertainment centre with a very varied programme of entertainment ranging from jazz and rock to serious theatre and musicals. A favourite haunt for some of Bristol's 22,000 students.

There are many other places of interest if you continue your walk along the harbourside but the star attraction has to be the SS *Great Britain*, the world's first ocean-going ship to be built of iron, designed by the great engineer, Isambard Kingdom Brunel, and launched in 1843. The ship is now being restored in the same dry dock where she was built and is an important tourist attraction.

On the opposite side of the harbour, you'll find the Pump House, which is a popular restaurant nowadays. In times gone by it was the main pumping station for the harbour.

For an easy and very enjoyable way of seeing the harbour, why not take a water tour? The *Bristol Packet* was originally a working narrowboat carrying coal in the north of England. Now it's a pleasure boat offering tours of the harbour and beyond.

You will now hear the recording again.

That is the end of Part 1.

Part 2

You will hear the details of a recipe. As you listen, complete the information for questions 11–18. Listen very carefully as you will hear the recording once only.

Today's recipe is for a delicious tomato and artichoke salad. It's very healthy – low in fat, high in fibre – and extremely quick and easy to prepare. The ingredients which follow are sufficient for four, but if you're cooking for fewer or more you can adjust the quantities accordingly. Now for the details ...

You'll need about 450 grammes of ripe tomatoes – make sure to test them for ripeness when you buy them. A 400 gramme can of artichoke hearts. A small onion. A large clove of garlic. The juice of half a lemon. About three tablespoons of olive oil – now that's about 45 millilitres if you're measuring exactly. Do make sure you use proper olive oil rather than a cheaper vegetable variety. 30 millilitres of fromage frais. Salt and pepper to taste and a few fresh sprigs of basil.

Now the method: First of all, you'll need to drain the artichoke hearts. Once you've done that, cut them in half. Next, quarter your tomatoes. And, when the main ingredients are prepared, arrange them on a suitable serving dish.

Now for the dressing. First you'll need to chop the onion roughly. Then crush the garlic and put it in a bowl along with the lemon juice, the oil, the fromage frais and the seasoning. Blend together well, using a whisk if possible. Once that's done, stir in the onion.

Finally, spoon the dressing over the prepared vegetables and the basil. Then cover the bowl and leave to chill in the refrigerator for about 30 minutes.

At only 110 calories per portion, this is a dish which should appeal to most slimmers. The salad should be prepared shortly before serving and it is not suitable for freezing.

That is the end of Part 2.

Part 3

You will hear some advice about interviews. For questions 19–28 complete each of the statements. You will hear the recording twice.

A Have you got any tips you could give me about interview techniques?

B Sure, well probably the most important thing is to make sure you get to the interview in the first place! And that depends on making a good application. You need to spend some time putting together your CV, that's, you know, a summary of your education, your qualifications, your past employment and so on. But keep it brief, preferably no more than one page long – you don't need to go into every detail – and make sure it's clear and well laid out. Type it, if you possibly can, or get someone to type it for you. Then you need to give an awful lot of thought to what you say in the covering letter. I mean, that's the first impression your potential boss will have of you, so it's pretty crucial. Find out as much as you can about the job and think about the kind of person they're likely to be looking for.

A Right.

B Don't forget to emphasise all the relevant experience you've had. If you work part-time in a shop, for example, you could say: 'I have a part-time job in retail which has improved my understanding of the business world.' You know, that sort of thing.

A And what about the interview itself?

B Now, in my experience, the most important thing about an interview is to prepare properly, to think of the different subject areas that you think you have some expertise in, and the different experiences that you've had that you want to get across to the interviewers and then make notes. Don't, whatever you do, just turn up at the interview and answer questions. I think that's a big mistake people make. They go in there without any clear idea of what they want to get across or what they want to tell the interviewers. If you do that, it'll be a one-sided interview, you'll answer questions and that'll be it. So do your preparation.

A Right.

B And somehow or other, when you're asked the

questions, incorporate the information into your answers. That way you have a little bit more control over the interview.

A But isn't there a danger they could think you were being too pushy?

B No, I didn't mean that you should come across like some kind of high-pressure salesperson, making a speech about how good you are! I don't think that would go down very well at all! No, the, the point is that the interviewer wants to hear you talk, so don't give monosyllabic answers to questions, say what you want to say but don't rabbit on too much either. Just be yourself, be natural, be interesting.

A What about your ... what you choose to wear on the big day? Is that important nowadays?

B Oh, I think it is, oh yeah. I think it's important to dress properly. There are varying degrees of just how well you can dress, of course, and it obviously depends quite a lot on the job you're going for. In the old days, it was a suit or nothing, but those days are gone. You can look very very smart without wearing a suit. Nice shirt, nice jumper, good pair of trousers, etc., etc. Be aware and make sure you're properly presented because that definitely makes a difference, especially if you're applying for a job where you'll be dealing with people, because they'll be looking for that.

A Right.

B Don't turn up in what you do the gardening in, for example.

A And if you're the kind of person who feels uncomfortable in a suit, it's probably best not to wear one, would you say?

B Yes, if you're going to feel uncomfortable, that would probably mean you don't perform well in the interview and that's a key point. An interview is a performance, well, that's what I think anyway. It's definitely a performance and if you feel uncomfortable, you won't perform well, and you won't get the job.

A That's been really useful. Thanks a lot.

B No problem. Good luck with the applications!

You will now hear the recording again.

That is the end of Part 3.

Part 4

You will hear five short extracts in which various people are talking about interview experiences. For questions 29–38, choose the correct option A, B or C. You will hear the recording twice.

1

It was the first interview I had for a teaching job. I didn't get it, incidentally, because the interview was particularly tricky. Anyway, I remember they asked me the question: 'Have you ever taught an advanced class?' and I said 'No'. And they said 'Do you find the idea daunting?' and I said 'Absolutely!' I realise now that perhaps I could have said 'Yes, I do find it daunting but it's also challenging, and I'd like to teach advanced classes because that's where a lot of interesting work is.' In other words, you can give the truth but you can qualify it.

2

And one interview I went to, they gave me a whole set of questions to answer and, when you've been in the trade for, you know, almost twenty years, you forget about all the academic side of things – you're just getting on with the work. I mean, if you give me a piece of rigging to fix – no problem. But ask me about Ohm's Law, and that's another story. And when I looked at the kind of questions they were, my mind just went blank. I didn't know what to do.

3

... and I walked in the room, and I'm a pretty casual kind of person and there was just four people sitting there on very high-backed chairs and about five feet away was my chair. And I sat there and everything that I'd thought about that I was going to say and all, how I was going to answer the questions, I just answered totally wrong, because I was just honest. And I'm the sort of person that if I feel something then I kind of show it. So I couldn't cover it up. And they were asking me things about, um, why had I sort of been away, because I'd been working abroad for six months. And I was saying, 'Oh, I love being abroad and I love travelling' and then I thought 'Oh, what am I saying? I'm not supposed to say that.'

4

Well, the man who interviewed me was, um, pretty aggressive from the word go and there was a point when he suddenly said: 'Spell the word "supersede".' So I spelt it. And he snorted and sort of pushed the dictionary across the desk – because we were in a classroom – and said 'Look it up'. Well, it is a tricky word! Anyway he then said, 'And you seriously think you can be a teacher?' So I said, 'I can always check spelling. I **know** I can teach'. Amazingly, I was successful in the end. I didn't really feel like working with the man but I needed the money!

5

A friend, I remember a friend of mine telling me about an interview that he went for with a really big multi-national company. And he was terribly nervous and he was sitting with a whole panel of people interviewing him, firing questions at him. But gradually, they brought him a cup of coffee and some biscuits, and he began to relax a little bit as he realised that the interview was going quite well. And as he really got into his stride, he completely forgot where he was and he dunked his biscuit in the coffee. And then he was expanding on a point and he stretched out his arm to make the point and bits of biscuit flew over the whole of the interviewing panel. He didn't get the job.

You will now hear the recording again.

That is the end of the test.

Test 4

Part 1

You will hear some advice about preventing car crime. For questions 1–10, fill in the missing information. You will hear the recording twice.

Speaker 1 Car crime is now a problem that affects us all, no matter where we live. Car thefts and thefts from cars make up almost a third of all reported crime. And about one in four of the cars reported missing each year is never recovered.

Speaker 2 Such statistics don't take account of the delay and inconvenience to you, the owner, if your car gets stolen. It can take a month or more before insurance claims are paid out, and if your car is returned to you, it may be badly damaged and in need of repair.

Speaker 1 Of all crimes, car crime is probably the most preventable. Simple and inexpensive measures can make an enormous difference in reducing the risk of your car becoming the next crime statistic.

Speaker 2 Keep your car safe!

Speaker 1 Don't leave luggage and valuables on display. Take them with you or lock them in the boot out of sight. And never leave credit cards in the glove compartment.

Speaker 2 Lock the doors **every** time you leave the car.

Speaker 1 Etch an identification number, such as your registration number, on to all glassware: the windows, head lamps and sunroof. Thieves won't want the expense of replacing them.

Speaker 2 Remove your ignition key even when your car is in the garage.

Speaker 1 Put your aerial down when you park.

Speaker 2 When you're choosing a radio cassette machine for the car, look for a security-coded model which won't work if somebody tampers with it. Or buy a machine which is specially designed so that it can be easily removed when you leave your car.

Speaker 1 Lockable wheel nuts are a sensible protection for expensive alloy wheels.

Speaker 2 If you have a lockable fuel cap, thieves will be forced to abandon your car when it runs out of petrol.

Speaker 1 Never leave vehicle documents in your car. Your registration document, MOT and insurance certificate could help a thief to sell your car.

Speaker 2 The safest place to park is your garage, if you have one. If you don't, choose your parking space carefully. A busy, well-lit area is the safest. Thieves don't want to risk being seen.

Speaker 1 You can get more information on crime prevention of all kinds by asking at your local police station for the leaflet called *Practical Ways to Crack Crime*.

Speaker 2 That was a public information announcement on behalf of the City Police.

You will now hear the recording again.

That is the end of Part 1.

Part 2

You will hear about a number of auction sales on a telephone information service. As you listen, complete the information for questions 11–19. Listen very carefully as you will hear the recording once only.

You have telephoned the Lloyds 24-hour recorded auction information service for sales at our Billingsgate office. Opening hours at this location are Mondays to Fridays between 9.00 a.m. and 5.30 p.m. and on Sunday, if applicable for special viewing, between 12 and 4.00 p.m.

Sales for the month of March are as follows:

Tuesday the 2nd of March: Old Master paintings at 10.30 a.m. in our large gallery.

Wednesday the 3rd of March: Silver and jewellery at 11.00 a.m., also in our large gallery. The showpiece of this sale is a magnificent matching set of diamond bracelet, brooch and wristwatch by Cartier.

Thursday the 4th of March: Books, atlases and maps at 11.30 a.m. in the Green Room.

Monday the 8th of March, European stamps at 2.00 p.m. in the Long Gallery. This sale includes several rare and important stamps, with estimates ranging from £100–£3,000.

Wednesday the 10th of March: Rock and pop memorabilia from the 50s and 60s at 10.00 a.m. in the large gallery.

Tuesday the 16th of March: Furniture and clocks at 11.00 a.m. The sale includes a large collection of 19th-century desks and bookcases.

Friday the 19th of March: Classic cars at 9.30 a.m. Please note that this sale will take place at Filton Airfield near Reading, not at our main offices.

Thursday the 25th of March: Toys and dolls at 2.30 p.m. in the Green Room. This sale features a number of doll's houses dating from the beginning of the century. There'll be Sunday viewing for this sale.

You can view sales for three days prior to the auction date. Catalogues can be purchased at the saleroom or ordered by telephone on our special catalogue Hot Line (071 543 2021).

Thank you for phoning the Lloyds auction information service.

That is the end of Part 2.

Part 3

You will hear part of an interview with a doctor on the subject of jet lag. For questions 20–29 complete each of the statements. You will hear the recording twice.

Interviewer Now let's turn to a problem connected with modern travel that gets mentioned quite a lot these days – jet lag. I looked it up in the dictionary before we came on the air and what the dictionary says is this: *a slight sense of confusion and tiredness that people experience after a long journey in an aeroplane, especially after arriving in a place where the time is different from the place they left.* Now, I've got Dr Leslie Blake here in the studio. Tell me, Leslie, does jet lag really exist or is it all in the mind?

Leslie Yes, I think it's certainly true to say that jet lag exists. Anybody who's done a long haul flight from, say, New York to Paris will know what we're talking about, anyway. Um, the problem is that the circadian rhythms ..

Interviewer Circadian rhythms?

Leslie Yes, these are the body rhythms that tell us when to eat and when to sleep and so on. These rhythms are affected by environmental cues – things like, er, clock hour and temperature and whether it's day or night.

Interviewer So what, what are the symptoms?

Leslie Well, you tend to have problems sleeping – you may fall asleep exhausted but then you wake up again three hours later in the middle of the night and lie awake for hours. You'll probably find that your eating patterns are disrupted so you have no appetite when everyone else is eating but you may be starving hungry at midnight! Um, the biggest problem, probably, is that one's performance, both mentally and physically, will be below par.

Interviewer So, it's not a good idea for a business executive to fly across the Atlantic for an important meeting and then go home?

Leslie No, no, not if he, or she, needs to be on top form. It may not be such a problem on a really flying visit where you don't really need to adapt to a new time zone – you're not there for long enough – but, generally speaking, um, recovering from jet lag normally takes about one day for each time zone that you've crossed. So, if you're going somewhere like Australia, you will need several days to recover before you're at peak efficiency again. And things like climate and even culture can make a difference to your recovery rate too. You may find it takes longer to adjust to things in Hong Kong, say, in summer than in Sydney in their winter.

Interviewer And are there remedies, anything we can take to prevent the effects of jet lag?

Leslie Anyone who could invent a remedy would become a millionaire! There are a few products on the market which promise to cure jet lag but there's no evidence that they work. Um, some people recommend carefully adjusting your sleeping patterns during the days before you leave so that you get used to sleeping later or earlier, whichever is closer to the time zone that you'll be going to. That may work but it's pretty impractical for most people. But there are a few simple things you can do which help. You can try to get some sleep on the aircraft, for example. It's also best to avoid heavy meals though that may be easier said than done – airlines do insist on waking you up to feed you at regular intervals, don't they?

Interviewer Yes, they do, it's maddening – but it's a way of passing the time, I suppose.

Leslie Yeah, on the whole, it's best to accept that you won't be feeling at your best for a while and to avoid important commitments for at least 24 hours after you arrive.

Interviewer So, some sensible advice on dealing with jet lag there from Dr Leslie Blake. Thanks, Leslie.

You will now hear the recording again.

That is the end of Part 3.

Part 4

You will hear five short extracts in which various people are talking about jet lag. For questions 30–39, choose the correct option A, B or C. You will hear the recording twice.

1

Well, I certainly suffer from jet lag when I go from, say, Australia to Britain, which is constantly flying backwards into yesterday. I think that jet lag isn't nearly as bad coming the other way, when you're flying east all the time. But there's not much you can do about that, is there? I find the journey is made a lot easier if you remember to drink lots of water on aeroplanes, to try to sleep before you get on the plane, and not to try to do it when you're already exhausted. That certainly helps.

2

And the other tip I find is, as soon as you get to your destination, try to get into the rhythms of the day there. So, even if you arrive there at 7 o'clock in the morning and you haven't had any sleep for 24 hours, try to go through the whole day without having a little nap or a rest, and then go to bed that evening. So that way you're getting into the new rhythm. It's hard. I've failed a couple of times, but I find from experience that's the best way to do it.

3

I, when I fly, if I'm tired at the end of a trip, I go to sleep no matter what time it is. I just crash. But other people try to stay up and, and go to bed when the sun goes down. And get up when the sun comes up. You dehydrate on board the aircraft, so it's advisable to take as much fluid as you possibly can, not alcoholic of course, but anything that's got plenty of sugar in it to, er, to build your stamina up. And try and eat reasonably balanced meals. No, no junk food.

4

… yes, certainly, it can be extremely tiring. There are times when I'm sitting up in the middle of the night trying to keep awake, wondering what on earth made me pick this career! I think, er, the answer is, er, that you at times have to force yourself to go to bed when you don't want to. And at other times you force yourself to get up when you don't want to – to make your body, sort of show the body who's boss, so that you get back into local time zone as quickly as possible.

5

I've tried a whole range of remedies for jet lag, including some pretty weird and wonderful ones, but funnily enough, it was my optician who gave me the most useful tips. He gave me some breathing exercises to do before and during the flight. Because apparently your breathing tends to be shallower on a plane. On his advice, I also avoid caffeine the day before the flight and, after landing, I take a brisk walk and then have a long bath, followed by a short nap. I wouldn't say they solve the problem completely, but they really seem to help.

You will now hear the recording again.

That is the end of the test.

Test 5

Part 1

You will hear an advertisement for a sale of household equipment. For questions 1–10, fill in the missing information. You will hear the recording twice.

Today and for the next seven days Snappy Super Stores are having a million pound clear-out. With thousands of items reduced by up to fifty per cent, 9 months free credit, **and** a range of unrepeatable free gifts and special offers, this is the sale you simply can't afford to miss!

Here are just some of the bargains on offer:

A Calypso colour television, the latest model with a 51 centimetre screen and remote control. Sale price £499 – a saving of £50. And that's not all. This magnificent television comes with a 4-year guarantee at no extra cost.

Fed up with washing up? Now's your chance to buy that dishwasher you've always wanted. The Dido Dish-o-matic takes twelve place settings comfortably and it costs an affordable £369. That's a saving of £10 on the recommended retail price. And that's not all. We're also offering a £50 cheque back. Ask at the store for details of this free cheque offer.

Next, save an incredible £150 on a new Olympus cooker. It has a double oven and a beautiful, easy-care ceramic hob. Sale price, just £649 and you'll have the chance of a free cruise too – ask at the store for details of this very special offer.

If you're concerned about economy and saving the planet, you can do your bit by buying a Pandora chest freezer. The Pandora is a low-energy model so it cuts down on bills and saves precious resources. We're offering it at the amazing price of just £369 – a saving of £60. Buy a freezer in the sale and you'll walk away with a free digital watch as well.

Lastly, is your vacuum cleaner past its best? Have you been thinking of replacing it? Well, now's your chance. The Luna Luxmaster is the vacuum cleaner which came out top in a recent consumer survey and it has the advantage of having built-in tools so you won't need to find somewhere to store them. The price is a ridiculous £99, which is a saving of £15 on the normal price. And free with the Luna Luxmaster is a personal stereo.

See these and thousands of other bargains in a Snappy Super Store near you. But hurry while stocks last!

You will now hear the recording again.

That is the end of Part 1.

Part 2

You will hear some advice on complaining about a holiday. As you listen, complete the information for questions 11–18. Listen very carefully as you will hear the recording once only.

Now, what do you do when your dream holiday turns out to be more of a nightmare? We look at how to deal with holiday complaints.

First of all, by far the best thing is to try and deal with any problems at the time, while you're still at the resort. So explain your complaint clearly to the company representative. He or she may well be able to sort out the problem there and then.

When you're packing, remember to take the brochure describing the holiday and also a copy of the booking form. They will provide evidence of what you've been promised, whether it's a sea view or an entertainment programme for the kids.

One very useful piece of equipment that you'll have with you is a camera. Use it to take photos of what you're complaining about: the condition of your room, for example, or the busy main road just in front of the hotel.

Keep all receipts for anything you have to spend to overcome the problems and make a note of the names and addresses of any other dissatisfied holidaymakers. It will be harder for the company to ignore a complaint if it's confirmed by several people.

Finally, make sure you fill in the tour operator's complaint form and give it to the representative. Keep a copy, too, for future reference.

After the holiday, write to the company as soon as possible – some companies have a time limit for complaints – and say how much compensation you are asking for. Work out the compensation by deciding how many days of your holiday were spoiled and then calculating what proportion that is of the total cost of the holiday.

And, if you still don't get satisfaction, you can contact ABTA, the Association of British Travel Agents, which operates an independent arbitration scheme for a registration fee of around £30.

If you would like our free fact sheet on Holiday Complaints, write to: 'Having a Lovely Time', Television House, London W2X 4LW.

That is the end of Part 2.

Part 3

You will hear part of an interview with Mary Dallas, an archaeologist whose work involves studying aboriginal sites in Australia. For questions 19–30 complete each of the statements. You will hear the recording twice.

Interviewer Would you say that you enjoy your job?
Mary Dallas Absolutely!
Interviewer And what about it makes it so enjoyable?
Mary Dallas It's, it's enjoyable because it's a combination of being out in the field wandering around in the bush and having that wonderful

outdoor type of life as well as sitting behind a desk and slogging away using your brain, etc.

Interviewer And how much time do you spend outside in the field?

Mary Dallas About a third, I think, of what I do.

Interviewer And two thirds following it up?

Mary Dallas Sitting at a desk, yes, being intelligent.

Interviewer And when you say 'walking around in the field', what does that mean? Does it mean literally?

Mary Dallas It does. Bush walking, bush walking in the … I would have to be looking for aboriginal sites in places that hadn't been greatly disturbed before, either by farming or by, um, suburbs, or residential or industrial, or whatever … So that I'm looking basically in places that haven't been – the bushland is generally intact. So it's like going for a nice bush walk.

Interviewer Do you go on your own, or how many people go?

Mary Dallas Oh, usually on my own. It depends. It depends on, um, I suppose, how rough it's going to be or whether it's going to be dangerous to be on your own or …

Interviewer What would make it dangerous?

Mary Dallas The ruggedness, I suppose, of the terrain, so that you would have, um, reason to worry about breaking a leg or falling down a cliff and then being on your own at the bottom of it. No one hearing you cry.

Interviewer What about animals? Snakes?

Mary Dallas Ah well, you see, you tend … I mean you can overestimate the, um, dangers in the bush but generally speaking I might see a snake two or three times a year, in all that time. You do see the dangerous ones, of course. But you don't …

Interviewer Which are the dangerous ones?

Mary Dallas In Australia, well they'd be tiger snakes and brown snakes and taipans up north.

Interviewer And have you always wanted to be an archaeologist?

Mary Dallas Since I was thirteen. Isn't that wonderful? I was one of these people that actually have always wanted to be an archaeologist instead of the ones who said, 'Gee, I wish I was one.' I went out and did it.

Interviewer And what at thirteen, what made you want to be an archaeologist?

Mary Dallas Oh in those days it was classical archaeology that I was much more interested in. I think I read a book on, um, Troy and that was the end of that. However, by the time I got to university,

the, the academic programmes at Sydney for archaeology consisted of classical archaeology, which was the straight Greek and Roman and Egyptian and Mesopotamian, and there was also an anthropology department which dealt with aboriginal culture and, and that one was simply far more interesting, so I went that way and left Greece and Rome behind.

Interviewer And what's the best preparation to be an archaeologist if you're at school, you're fifteen years old and you're interested in …

Mary Dallas Oh, if I could do it all over again, how would I become a better one? I think I'd probably do a lot more geology and geomorphology and natural science subjects. And it was, in the degree at Sydney, it was extremely difficult to do that because the, the degree is part of an Arts course and in those days, this is a hundred years ago we're talking about, the, the science subjects were separated out pretty well. And if you wanted to do a science subject, you pretty well had to do a separate degree along with your Arts one, so it was very difficult then.

Interviewer And what about opportunities for women? Is it, um, is it a field that it's difficult for women to get into?

Mary Dallas Traditionally it was the – just about the only people who enrolled in the degree courses were women. And that was because there were so few career opportunities and it was, I mean in other words if you wanted to make money you went off and did law or you went off and did medicine. And archaeology wasn't seen as anything other than an academic pursuit. And in fact anthropology at Sydney University, Anthropology 1 was known as Marriage 1 – there's one in every university, I'm sure. So that you, you went off to find your husband by doing Anthropology 1. So that women did, women did it as a, um, not so much as a career event but they, but as soon as it became a lucrative profession in, in the consulting area, suddenly the, the field is full of young boys expecting to make their fame and fortune, you see. But it's too late. We have the market cornered! All us older women.

You will now hear the recording again.

That is the end of Part 3.

Part 4

You will hear five short extracts in which various people are talking about speeches they have heard. Task one. For questions 31–35, match the extracts as you hear them with the occasions when the speeches were made, listed A–H. Task two. For questions 36–40, match the extracts as you hear them with the aspects of the speeches that were impressive, listed A–H. Remember you must complete both tasks as you listen. You will hear the recording twice.

1

Yes, and the thing about this speech that the bridegroom was giving was that he did it completely off the cuff. It didn't seem to be a prepared speech at all. He just stood up and started speaking and he had all the guests' attention immediately because it was so natural and direct. Normally when people give speeches, they're looking down a lot of time, aren't they, reading sort of prompt cards? Because I think the very best speakers often don't have their speech written out, do they, and that's what makes them so effective. Maybe they just have good memories or maybe they're just natural performers …

2

And the other speech, if I can go on for a minute, was given by a man that works with me, not a professional speaker or anything. And he gave a speech to about 400, 500 of our colleagues who'd gathered to say good-bye to our boss who was retiring. And Bill had the boss to a T, you know, the way he was talking about our old boss was exactly as the boss was. And it was funny and it was witty. And we were rolling about! It was great, it really was!

3

I belong to our local Women's Institute and we get all sorts of speakers at our meetings but one we had recently was superb. I forget what the title was now but she made her point by telling a story – all about a train journey she'd made and everything that happened. I won't tell it now because it would take too long but it kept us all listening because she made it so interesting and we wanted to know what happened next and we didn't realise until the very end what the point, the moral, was. It was very effective.

4

Years ago my eldest son went to a school where the head teacher had that ability to make a really good speech. I'll never forget when he first went there, there was a meeting where the head addressed all the new children and their parents. And it's quite a big thing, isn't it, when your child makes these giant steps in their life? The speech was really moving and by the end of that little assembly, I mean, even the men in the audience were sniffing and snuffling into their handkerchiefs. I think the really good speakers are the ones who can bring a tear to your eye and make you think as well.

5

I'm president of the Rotary Club and one thing we're very anxious about is to encourage young people in the ability to speak in public. And therefore we hold a public speaking competition every year for schoolchildren of under 16. And it's a source of wonder to me that these young people can get up and talk for ten minutes and do it so well. I can remember clearly one young man who spoke to us – it was something to do with workers' rights – and he was so fired with his very strong views that we could all see him as a future Secretary General of a trade union.

You will now hear the recording again.

That is the end of the test.

▶ Answer Key

Practice Test 2

Paper 1

Part 1

1 C	6 A	11 A	15 E
2 E	7/8 D/E	12 C	16 A
3/4 A/D	9 C	13 F	
5 B	10 D	14 B	

Part 2

17 F	19 G	21 D
18 A	20 B	22 C

Part 3

23 C	25 A	27 B
24 C	26 D	28 A

Part 4

29/30 E/F	31/32 B/C	33/34 F/G	35 A
36 G	37 D	38 G	39 A
40/41 D/E	42 B	43/44 A/D	45 F
46 E	47/48 A/F		

Paper 3

Part 1

0 D (example)

1 A	5 A	9 D	13 D
2 B	6 B	10 A	14 B
3 D	7 A	11 C	15 C
4 C	8 B	12 C	

Part 2

0 by (example)

16 in	20 Had	24 as	28 in
17 instead	21 with	25 will	29 has
18 Between	22 what	26 if	30 of
19 returning	23 apart	27 so	

Part 3

0 days. It (example)
0 expenses (example)
0 ✓ (example)

31 specially	39 hundreds
32 reference	40 manufacturers, realising
33 journalists, cannot	41 ✓
34 facilities	42 women
35 ✓	43 efficient
36 computer	44 four-drawer
37 ✓	45 ✓
38 establish	46 hardly

Part 4

0 icy (example)

47 loss	52 fascination	57 childhood
48 sinking	53 global	58 surely
49 legendary	54 emotional	59 spectacular
50 consciousness	55 surprisingly	60 creative
51 survivors	56 courteous	61 relationship(s)

Part 5

0 or more (example)   **62 judged**   **63 experts**
64 appear/be printed/be published   65 value
66 total/all   67 minimum
68 must complete/use
69 closing date/final date/deadline   70 returned
71 accompanied   72 a suitable/an appropriate
73 announced/listed   74 responsibility

Part 6

0 J (example)

75 G	77 I	79 C
76 D	78 A	80 E

Paper 4

Part 1

1 (the) announcement   2 leave/record a message
3 another (tele)phone   4 for business
5 good value   6 saving space
7 (rather/a bit) complicated
8 crystal-clear; very/extremely clear
9 (a bit/slightly) over-priced

Part 2

10 sandwiches	14 comfortable clothing
11 the (swimming) pool	15 (about) 3 hours
12 (the) gold market	16 (about) 4 o'clock/p.m.
13 musical entertainment	17 afternoon tea

Part 3

18 C	20 D	22 B	24 A
19 B	21 D	23 C	

Part 4

25 F	28 D	31 E	34 F
26 E	29 A	32 C	
27 H	30 D	33 A	

Practice Test 3

Paper 1

Part 1

1 D	6 E	11 H	15/16/17 A/C/I
2/3 G/J	7/8 B/F	12 E	
4 B	9 J	13 G	
5 I	10 C	14 J	

Part 2

18 G		20 A		22 B	
19 D		21 F		23 C	

Part 3

24 D		26 A		28 C	
25 B		27 C		29 B	

Part 4

30 C	35 A	41/42 A/B	48 A
31 B	36/37 C/E	43 D	49 E
32 E	38 A	44 B	
33 A	39 E	45 E	
34 D	40 D	46/47 C/E	

Paper 3

Part 1

0 B (example)

1 B	5 D	9 A	13 C
2 C	6 B	10 D	14 A
3 A	7 D	11 A	15 D
4 C	8 C	12 B	

Part 2

0 has (example)

16 the/any	21 could	26 and
17 being	22 over/across	27 be
18 as	23 those	28 on
19 in	24 into	29 will
20 Anyone	25 it	30 with

Part 3

0 ✓ (example)
0 lives (example)

31 the	37 all	43 which
32 been	38 ✓	44 of
33 it	39 will	45 ✓
34 and	40 up	46 over
35 about	41 that	
36 ✓	42 ✓	

Part 4

0 extinction (example)

47 chairman/chairperson	55 geographical
48 unveiled	56 environmental
49 holidaymakers	57 accompanied
50 armfuls	58 explanation
51 ecologically	59 informative
52 equipped	60 confusion
53 outdated	61 depressing
54 extensive	

Part 5

0 unable (example)

62 attend	69 raise/increase
63 be held/take place	70 seems to/appears to
64 matters/business/affairs	71 result in/lead to
65 agreed/offered	72 reduction/decrease
66 place	73 in favour
67 report	74 introduce/impose
68 support/agree with	

Part 6

0 J (example)

75 F	76 H	77 A
78 C	79 G	80 E

Paper 4

Part 1

1 water sports	6 entertainment centre
2 storage shed	7 tourist attraction
3 media centre	8 pumping station
4 tea warehouse	9 (popular) restaurant
5 arts centre	10 pleasure boat

Part 2

11 4/four (people)	15 serving dish
12 ripe	16 in a bowl
13 olive oil	17 30 minutes
14 cut (them) in half	18 for freezing

Part 3

19 one/1 page/side (long)	24 control over/of
20 covering letter	25 high-pressure
21 relevant experience	26 wear a suit
22 make notes	27 dealing with people
23 one-sided	28 perform/do well

Part 4

29 B	32 C	35 B	38 B
30 C	33 A	36 A	
31 A	34 C	37 B	

Practice Test 4

Paper 1

Part 1

1 F	6 B	11 B	16 E
2/3 C/E	7/8 A/E	12 A/H	17 F
4 C	9 B	13/14 H	18 A
5 G	10 G	15 D	

Part 2

19 D	20 B	21 G	22 A	23 C	24 F

Part 3

25 D   26 B   27 C   28 C   29 A   30 B

Part 4

31 E	36 B	42 E	48/49 A/B
32/33 B/C	37/38 A/D	43/44 B/C	
34 A	39/40 C/E	45/46 A/D	
35 D	41 B	47 C	

Paper 3

Part 1

0 C (example)

1 C	4 A	7 B	10 A	13 B
2 B	5 A	8 B	11 D	14 A
3 D	6 C	9 D	12 C	15 D

Part 2

0 an (example)

16 on	20 were	24 to	28 to
17 Within	21 from	25 on	29 the
18 After	22 while	26 from	30 something
19 could	23 to	27 made	

Part 3

0 ✓ (example)
0 television, video (example)
0 Government (example)

31 actions, if	39 ✓
32 effect	40 a lot," said
33 ✓	41 Environment
34 appliances	42 ✓
35 they're	43 targets
36 standby, will	44 home, the
37 ✓	45 Retailing
38 gadget	46 steel

Part 4

0 medical (example)

47 happiness	55 especially
48 beneficial	56 behaviour
49 laughter	57 cheerfulness
50 conventional	58 catching
51 youngsters	59 unrewarding
52 muscular	60 suspicious
53 facial	61 lively
54 sadness	

Part 5

0 job (example)
62 a waitress
63 taking (down)/writing down
64 dishes
65 a hand

66 a while
67 the weekend/(the) weekends
68 four-hour
69 meeting/talking to
70 cool
71 right
72 before
73 any/the tips
74 a call/a ring

Part 6

0 J (example)

75 I	77 A	79 G
76 F	78 C	80 E

Paper 4

Part 1

1 inconvenience	6 in the garage
2 preventable	7 easily removed
3 on display	8 abandon
4 credit cards	9 sell the/your car/it
5 an identification/your registration	10 well-lit

Part 2

11 12–4 p.m.	16 Airfield
12 Silver and jewellery	17 doll's houses
13 European stamps	18 3/three days
14 £3,000	19 (a) catalogue(s)
15 Furniture and clocks	

Part 3

20 confusion (and) tiredness	25 (the) culture
21 temperature	26 no evidence
22 sleeping	27 get some sleep/sleep
23 performance	28 (eating) heavy meals
24 time zone	29 (at least) 24 hours

Part 4

30 B	33 B	36 C	39 B
31 A	34 A	37 B	
32 C	35 C	38 A	

Practice Test 5

Paper 1

Part 1

1 E	6/7 C/E	12 E	17/18 B/C
2 F	8 A	13 D	
3/4 A/B	9/10 B/C	14/15 C/E	
5 D	11 F	16 E	

Part 2

19 C	21 B	23 A
20 F	22 G	24 E

Part 3

25 B	27 A	29 B	31 C
26 A	28 D	30 C	

Part 4

32 F	36 A	40 D	44/45 E/F
33 D	37 E	41 D	46 E
34 C	38 D	42 F	
35 F	39 F	43 B	

Paper 3

Part 1

0 D (example)

1 C	5 C	9 C	13 D
2 B	6 A	10 D	14 C
3 A	7 B	11 A	15 C
4 D	8 B	12 B	

Part 2

0 in (example)

16 In/Within	21 goes/is	26 like
17 All	22 for	27 both
18 without	23 will	28 the
19 some/many	24 held/set	29 However
20 to	25 for	30 on

Part 3

0 to (example)

0 ✓ (example)

31 which	35 ✓	39 had	43 was
32 the	36 a	40 ✓	44 ✓
33 ✓	37 if	41 able	45 the
34 be	38 not	42 for	46 are

Part 4

0 identifiable (example)

47 novelist	55 achievements
48 variety	56 mathematicians
49 perception(s)	57 discovery
50 excellence	58 absence
51 Courageously	59 immobile
52 absorbing	60 observation
53 revelations	61 overlooked
54 numerous	

Part 5

0 inform you (example)

62 attention
63 inspected/visited
64 behalf
65 aware of / informed/warned about
66 pointed
67 leak
68 safety/health
69 replacing/mending
70 cleaning
71 constantly/continuously
72 undertake/do/organise
73 delay
74 alternative

Part 6

0 J (example)

75 F	77 G	79 D
76 C	78 I	80 A

Paper 4

Part 1

1 remote control	6 free cruise
2 4-year guarantee	7 low-energy
3 Dishwasher	8 (digital) watch
4 £50 cheque back	9 Vacuum cleaner
5 double oven	10 personal stereo

Part 2

11 representative	15 confirmed
12 booking form	16 a copy
13 (the) condition	17 compensation
14 overcome	18 registration fee

Part 3

19 at/behind a desk	25 13/thirteen
20 a/one third	26 classical
21 farming	27 at university
22 rough (or) dangerous	28 (natural) science
23 breaking a leg	29 Marriage 1/One
24 snakes	30 men/young boys

Part 4

31 D	34 H	37 A	40 B
32 F	35 E	38 D	
33 A	36 F	39 E	